LANGUAGE OF AUTISTIC CHILDREN

LANGUAGE OF AUTISTIC CHILDREN

DON W. CHURCHILL
Indiana University School of Medicine

1978

V. H. WINSTON & SONS
Washington, D.C.

A HALSTED PRESS BOOK

JOHN WILEY & SONS
New York   Toronto   London   Sydney

V. H. Winston & Sons, a Division of Scripta Technica, Inc., Publishers
1511 K Street, N.W., Washington, D.C. 20005

Distributed solely by Halsted Press, a Division of John Wiley & Sons, Inc.

Library of Congress Cataloging in Publication Data

Churchill, Don W.   1930—
    Language of autistic children.

    1. Autism.   2. Mentally ill children—Language.
I. Title
RJ506.A9C47   618.9'28'982   78-18860
ISBN 0-470-26417-9

Composition by **Maria A. Maddalena**, Scripta Technica, Inc.

TO MY MOTHER AND FATHER

CONTENTS

PREFACE

In writing this book, I have been reminded at times of the schoolboy whose book report read, "This book tells more about penguins than I care to know." Perhaps this book tells more about the speech and language of autistic children than you care to know. This prospect presents a dilemma. Possibly it is the dilemma of seeing the forest and the trees at once. For on the one hand, the data seem to allow generalizations which should hold interest for a diverse group—clinicians, linguists, parents, educators. On the other hand, the import of these generalizations can be appreciated only by painstaking attention to the minute observations from which they are derived. Close attention to such a mountain of detail is bound to be tedious for some. Although I have struggled mightily to provide some relief here and there by way of speculations, reviews, and bits of human interest, the mountain of detail remains, and I have been unwilling to reduce the data further than I already have. I am convinced that appreciation of those matters of more general import—whereby autistic children are both linked to and distinguishable from nonautistic children—cannot be properly appreciated unless the reader has dug here and there into the raw data. The book may best be read in small doses. My hope is that those who can endure a bit of tedium will break through the dry facts into the fascination and wonder of viewing a vital aspect of autistic children up close.

1

This work was supported in part by Public Health Service Grant MH-05154 from the National Institute of Mental Health and in part by Carter Memorial Hospital, State of Indiana. I wish to acknowledge the steady support of the hospital's Medical Director, Donald F. Moore, M.D., and of my colleagues, Marian K. DeMyer, M.D. and Joseph N. Hingtgen, Ph.D., as well as the help of my research assistant, Mrs. Clara Pinkney. Most especially, I am indebted and grateful to and admiring of the staff of the Research Unit: Jesse Patterson, Joyce Cork, Luvenia Davis, Jackie Fuqua, Nora O'Bannon, Carolyn Cadwallader, Martha Anderson, Margaret Hall, Mort Smith, Betty Horton, Faye Warfield, and Ruth Sparks. How these people, day after day, combined such sensitive responsiveness to children with such dogged persistence in the face of all too commonly discouraging results amazed me then, and does still. It may have been that we kept each other going, but in any case it is clear that the work presented here could not have been done without them. Carol S. Sproles for months and years had faithfully typed and typed and typed, uncannily decoding my inserts and tortuous arrows, at times volunteering more than I in good conscience could ask for. Finally, for the preparation of the index and help in reading proof I wish to thank Susan K. Tibbals.

Don W. Churchill, M.D.
April, 1978

CHAPTER 1

INTRODUCTION

This monograph began as a chapter in a book project summing up and integrating 10 years of biological, psychological, and demographic research at the Clinical Research Center for Early Childhood Schizophrenia, Indianapolis, Indiana.[1] The chapter material outgrew that book project. Because language function is now recognized as such an important aspect—perhaps the most important aspect—of the syndrome of early infantile autism and, to my knowledge, nothing like the research presented here has been done elsewhere, and also because rather detailed presentation of the results of this work is essential to evaluating its significance, it has seemed prudent to allow the material to grow into a monograph rather than to prune it to the confines of a chapter in which, necessarily, the reader could do little more than view a general outline of procedures and results and be asked to accept someone else's inferences. The work was done in a setting of program research, heartily

[1] A significant portion of the Clinical Research Center's 10-year effort will appear in book form. DeMyer, Marian K. *Autistic Children and Their Parents.* Washington, D.C.: V. H. Winston & Sons, in press.

funded, with an entire hospital ward and all its supporting staff enjoying relative freedom from any claims competing with the narrow, primary mission of systematically studying and treating children of our choice. The support for enterprises such as that has now, of course, drastically changed, which is only one reason why it seems unlikely that the work presented here will soon be repeated.

Readers unfamiliar with the syndrome of early infantile autism may consult Kanner's (1943) original description and the more recent excellent reviews by Rutter (1968, 1971, 1978a). Here it need only be noted that the essential features of infantile autism include lack of speech for communication, a profound affective withdrawal and attendant severe impairment of human relationships, little or no appropriate use of objects, while at the same time manifesting an "obsessive concern with sameness," as seen in highly stereotyped or ritualistic behavior. Finally, the age of onset is always prior to 30 months, i.e., it is an early onset psychosis (Kolvin, 1971). Although for decades the condition was considered to be the result of bad mothering, there are few who continue to hold that view; rather, there is now very strong evidence that these children suffer some neurobiological impairment. At the level of psychological investigation, there has been increasing attention in recent years to the effect of this impairment on the language of autistic children. Hence, this book.

Diagnosis is crucial and has often received too little attention in published studies. All of the children reported on in this book were scrupulously diagnosed as autistic (with some exceptions to be noted) according to the criteria stated above. The particular diagnostic procedure used with these children has been compared with four other diagnostic systems (DeMyer, Churchill, Pontius, & Gilkey, 1971) and has been found to be in good accord with other carefully diagnosed groups of autistic children. Of the 16 children[2] whose language skills were evaluated with the experimental 9-word language, 13 had been diagnosed autistic. Speech ability ranged from muteness to echolalia to jargon with some functional speech. Two were not autistic but were mentally subnormal. One had an expressive aphasia. All but two of the children were boys, and of these all were white except for two who were black and one who was of mixed Oriental and European extraction. At the mid-point of their work with the experimental 9-word language, their ages ranged from 59 to 108 months with a mean age of 74 months. The selection of these particular autistic children, from among 175 so diagnosed, was largely a function of which children happened to be hospitalized on the Research

---

[2]Individual case studies are presented in detail in Chap. 4 for 14 of these children; two studies (one low-functioning autistic boy and one low-functioning autistic girl) have been excluded primarily due to redundancy and lack of comprehensive data. Each child's diagnostic category and level of functioning is presented on page 131.

Unit during the time of these studies. They were not selected for admission simply to participate in these language studies. Of those children hospitalized, there was, however, deliberate inclusion of autistic children in the lowest, middle, and highest ranges of functioning, as well as of some children who had not been diagnosed autistic. A thumbnail sketch of each child is presented in Chapter 4. But first, there follows a brief discussion of language in relation to infantile autism.

CHAPTER 2

LANGUAGE IN RELATION TO AUTISM

Language disability must occupy a central place in any consideration of infantile autism. This is so whether the approach is purely descriptive or is one of rational analysis. From the descriptive standpoint, one of the most striking features of the autistic child is impaired language: He communicates poorly or not at all, either by word or by gesture. In terms of rational analysis, it is more parsimonious to postulate a single disability underlying those symptoms which are common to all autistic children (although the causes of that disability may vary among children) than to assume that there are several independent disabilities making separate contributions to a single symptom complex. Language would appear to be one area of functioning which is comprehensive and influential enough in normal development so as to require serious consideration.

This is not to say that language impairment need be the only handicap of autistic children; indeed, there is considerable evidence that many autistic children have impairments of perception, memory, or motor skills as well. These additional impairments may account for some of the diversity of functioning found among autistic children. Nevertheless, it is reasonable to inquire whether the critical signs of autism, i.e., those signs which are common to *all* autistic children, may not be a manifestation of an underlying impairment of language function. There is the distinct possibility that such language impairment is a nessary and sufficient proximate cause of infantile autism.

Clarification of the word "language" is in order. First, it is important to distinguish between language and speech. Humans speak; so do parrots. Humans have language; parrots do not. Putting it differently, speech is regarded here as the ability to emit sounds which can be recognized as words. Examples of speaking birds are familiar to everyone. Clinicians, such as neurologists and speech therapists, know that patients with particular diseases may produce recognizable words which serve no language function. Conversely, some patients are unable to speak but give abundant evidence of language ability through writing or gestures. This, of course, is observable at any moment in the imaginative play of normal children, even though no words may be spoken. Also, some deaf individuals have no speech but communicate via manual sign language.

Language, then, refers to a more complex, abstract, and comprehensive function than does speech. While speech may be the commonest manifestation of language, it is not essential. Language refers to the meaningful association between signs or symbols—either spoken words, written symbols, gestures, or play/work sequences—which are essential to communication. It has been our experience with autistic children that their speech may or may not be impaired, but their language is always impaired—and very seriously so. Indeed, it is our impression that the severity of autistic impairment is correlated with the severity of this language impairment, and that the progress made by an autistic child, not only in the area of communication but in the manner of relating to others and competency of object use as well, is correlated with the degree to which this deficient language function is recoverable either in the course of spontaneous development and maturation or (less likely) through remedial therapy.

Two other assumptions should be made explicit. The first is that development of language is based on inherent biological capabilities of the organism and requires more than conditioning for its full development. Increasing appreciation of the enormous language capacity of humans has made efforts to explain this function solely on the basis of conditioning quite inadequate. Language capacity rests with the organism and will be expressed, given minimal environmental support, far beyond what can be accounted for on the basis of conditioning alone. The second assumption is that language, whether expressed in speech or otherwise, depends on precision skills which are normally apparent at an early age. Such skills anchor the far-ranging performance of later language development. These precision skills include the ability to make subtle sensory discriminations accurately and consistently, to associate certain stimuli with each other accurately and consistently, and to transfer information "bits" across various input and output channels. For example, receptively a child must be able to make a consistent visual discrimination between a spoon and a shoe, a consistent auditory discrimination between "spoon" and "shoe," and to regularly associate these sounds and sights in one way only. Expressively, similar demands for accurate and consistent discriminations and associations must be made if a child is to be readily understood. The child's later ability to abstract, classify, and use these words metaphorically does not obviate these requirements. These simple but precise skills, while not adequate to explain full language functioning, are nevertheless logical prerequisites of it. Further, the conditioning model, despite its limitations in a comprehensive consideration of language, may well be adequate to explain the acquisition of these underlying precision skills. Thus, this "basic conditionability" may be viewed as a necessary condition of normal language development, but it is not sufficient.

CHAPTER 3

THE EXPERIMENTAL 9-WORD LANGUAGE

STRATEGY

Overall, our method was devised to cast as wide and fine-meshed a net as possible in examining the language function of autistic children. We start from the simplest of conditionable performances and extend hierarchically upward through the ability to manipulate syntactic structure, deal with symbols, and finally to generate and understand novel sentences. While our overall procedures span this whole range, the experimental 9-word language (9WL) presented here represents only the lower end of this continuum. By means of the 9WL, we examine the basic conditionability of auditory and visual input channels and speech and motor output channels, as well as the connections between these, the ability to generalize beyond particular stimuli to classes of stimuli, and to cross-reference. Although the integrity of these basic functions does not guarantee full language competence, we infer it to be prerequisite to such competence. From the outset, we have attempted to look intensively at individual children rather than to derive group data. One implication of this is that control cases are not part of the design; rather, to the degree possible, each child has served as his own control, an approach which seems fitting in view of the material and methods. We have paid attention to each child's performance abilities and disabilities and especially to his *error patterns*, which are usually consistent and "reasonable," and often suggest new ways to facilitate learning. But the analysis of error patterns requires very close inspection of performance—often trial-by-trial—and lends itself poorly to statistical summary. Finally, the procedures as such are based on a kind of "limit testing," i.e., it is assumed that at the time of measurement the child is displaying his best performance under given conditions.[3]

PROCEDURE

An experimental 9-word language (9WL), adpated from the schemata of Mark (1969), was developed in the course of diagnostic treatment in an effort to more precisely identify points at which children failed to develop functional language. Basically it consists of a technique for examining single channels of information input and output, and associations across channels. Beginning with extremely simple stimuli, the 9WL progresses upward to integrations of increasing complexity. Receptive auditory, receptive visual, expressive speech and expressive motor functions are initially tested, starting with a single stimulus. The nine words of the 9WL consist of three nouns, three adjectives, and three verbs. By eventually presenting stimuli in a series of two parts of speech, and finally three, it is possible to present a series of three-word sentences, i.e., a simplified grammar. Using hand signs and also words, it is possible to examine auditory and visual receptive channels independently, as well as speech and motor expressive channels. A generalization test is done for each function to test whether a child can not only make cross-modal associations (conditioning), but also to see if there is some capacity to abstract or generalize to novel stimuli. The last step in the 9WL is to test cross-referencing ability. We then move beyond the 9WL to tasks which include other elements of linguistic structure such as prepositions and pronouns. Finally, the procedure uses structured "conversation" to

---

[3]This is important for those who impute to autistic children phobic avoidance or willful withholding of performance which they might readily display under more felicitous circumstances. Nothing in several years of experience in working with the children to be described would support this contention. To the contrary, the methods employed, the behavioral indicators of motivation and attitudes of the children, and the usual reliable performances on language tasks strongly imply that these children are giving close to their best performance under the circumstances of measurement. This point has been made previously (Churchill, 1969, 1971; Hingtgen, Coulter, & Churchill, 1967; Hingtgen & Churchill, 1969).

examine the child's ability to generate and understand novel sentences. The overall design is such that no child should be incapable of consistently performing some of the simplest tasks and, if he progresses through the most complex tasks, it can be safely inferred that he is capable of generative language.[4]

DESCRIPTION

In developing the 9WL, initially pictures or small toys were used as stimuli, but it was soon apparent that these stimuli were too complex and/or ambiguous for most autistic children. To simplify things the following stimuli were selected:

> Nouns were represented by three blocks (2 in. cubes), three sticks (5/8 X 6 in. dowels, and three rings (wooden curtain rings: 2-¾ in. outside diameter, 1-¾ in. inside diameter).
> Adjectives were represented by the colors red, blue, and yellow (each object within a noun-set being painted one of these colors).
> Verbs were represented by the actions "tap," "slide," "give."

The nine words of the experimental language could then be signified either vocally (block, stick, ring; red, blue, yellow; tap, slide, give) or by distinct hand signs. For the latter, a closed fist, an upheld index finger, and a circle formed by touching the tips of the thumb and forefinger represented *block, stick,* and *ring,* respectively.

> *Red* was represented by flat downturned palms crossing back and forth once.
> *Yellow* was represented by flat opposed palms 6 in. apart, moving downward once.
> *Blue* was represented by simply folding one's hands on the table.
> *Give* was represented by a flat upturned palm.
> *Tap* was represented by the right fingers straight, together and pointing down, tips touching the table.
> *Slide* was represented by the right palm downturned near the table.

When a child had mastered all nine words individually in any modality, a generalization test was given employing that same modality. Then, again using the original nine objects, he could progress to 2-word and finally 3-word

---

[4]No autistic child tested to date has demonstrated full capacity on this range of tasks. Sooner or later each reaches an apparent impasse.

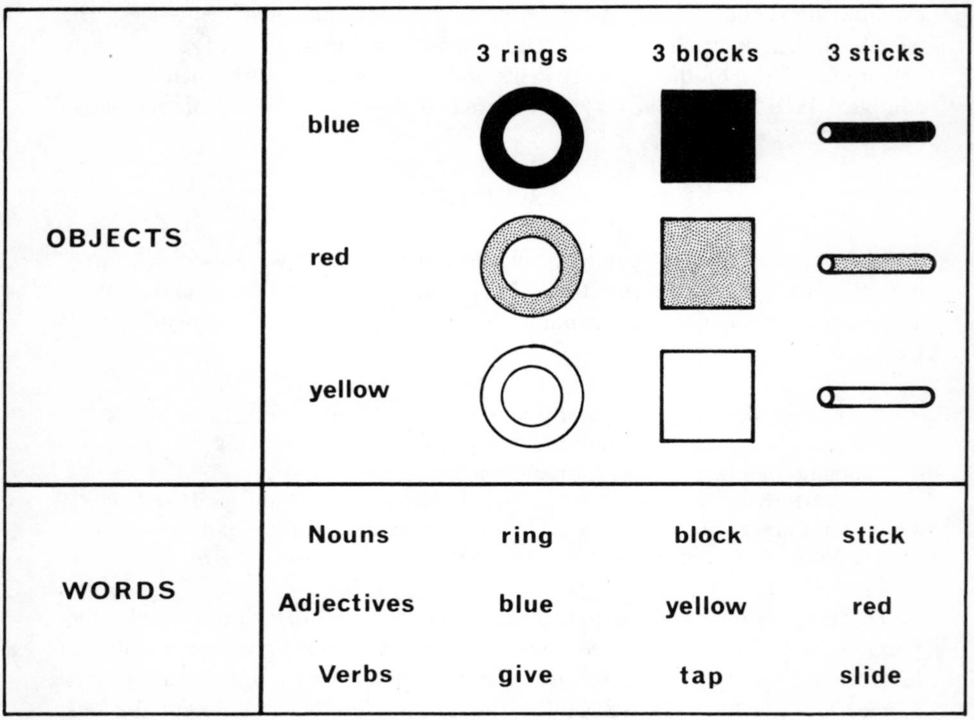

FIG. 1. Nine objects and nine words used in experimental 9WL.

combinations in that modality. Thus, he would eventually be dealing with simple sentences such as "Tap red stick" and "Give blue ring." For children progressing that far, it still was possible to test, relatively[5] independently, auditory and visual receptive functions as well as speech and motor expressive functions.

The last part of the 9WL consisted of "cross-referencing" tasks. Any of the nine objects possessed simultaneously two potentially relevant stimulus dimensions, i.e., shape and color. Thus, if a red block were held up, the examiner might ask for the child to say (or sign) *either* the shape *or* the color, whereupon a correct response would consist of only "block" or "red," respectively. This performance too could be tested across modalities

---

[5] To the author's knowledge no task has ever been devised which tests only a single sensory or motor function.

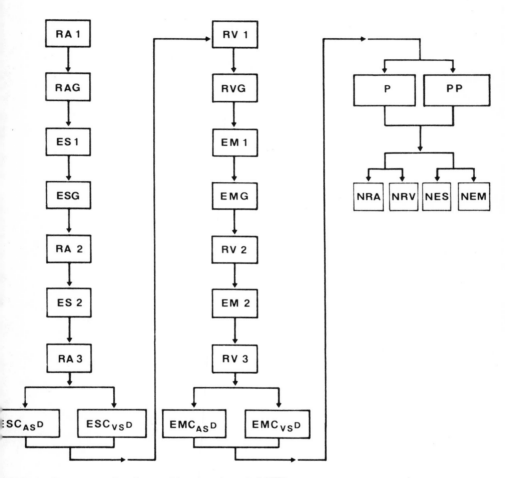

FIG. 2. Sequence of tasks used in experimental 9WL.

Legend: Numerals refer to number of words in task. R = receptive; E = expressive; A = auditory; V = visual; S = speech; M = motor; G = generalization (novel stimuli); C = cross-referencing; S^D = discriminative stimulus; P = pronouns; PP = prepositions; NRA = novel sentences: following directions; NRV = reading novel sentences; NES = describing novel situations; NEM = writing novel sentences.

CHILD _____   E _____   R _____

DATE _____.

TIME: Start _____ Stop_____

TASK _____

Trial	Stimulus	Response	Trial	Stimulus	Response	Trial	Stimulus	Response
1			26			51		
2			27			52		
3			28			53		
4			29			54		
5			30			55		
6			31			56		
7			32			57		
8			33			58		
9			34			59		
10			35			60		
11			36			61		
12			37			62		
13			38			63		
14			39			64		
15			40			65		
16			41			66		
17			42			67		
18			43			68		
19			44			69		
20			45			70		
21			46			71		
22			47			72		
23			48			73		
24			49			74		
25			50			75		
	Success/Trial			Success/Trial			Success/Trial	

FIG. 3. Sample data sheet.

depending upon whether the discriminative stimulus was auditory or visual and whether a speech or motor response was required.

The planned sequence of tasks used in the experimental 9-word language is shown in Figure 2. This plan was modified as necessary to accommodate the special problems or abilities of individual children. Following out this sequence usually required about 3 months with each child even when three sessions each day were scheduled. Sessions of 75 trials could normally be completed in 20 to 45 minutes. Recording was done by the adult after each trial using a standard form and designated symbols.

In each session the adult would sit facing the child, with a small table between them. When the child was quiet and watching the adult, a discriminative stimulus was given. A response within 5 seconds was immediately followed by verbal feedback, and, if correct, a small food reinforcer. For some children, sessions were scheduled so that they would be working for bites of their three regular meals each day. If motivation was high enough and responding was regular, between-meal snacks were sufficiently reinforcing to maintain regular responses. Schedules of reinforcement could be adjusted any time as needed. The overall goal was simply to maintain a cooperative and attentive response set, relying as much as possible on secondary (social) reinforcers or any reinforcement which might he inherent in the task itself. In test sessions (as opposed to training sessions), no food reinforcers were used.

A typical session consisted of three blocks of 25 trials. Although procedures for testing sessions were rigidly specified, procedures during the training sessions were left as flexible as possible, so long as they remained in the operant conditioning paradigm. For instance, a correction procedure was ordinarily used in training sessions, i.e., following an incorrect response the same discriminative stimulus was presented until the child made the correct response. Prompts, even to the point of "forcing" correct responses, were used as needed, with the prompt gradually being faded on successive trials. While some children had no difficulty dealing with all nine stimulus objects from the outset, correct responding was facilitated in other children by limiting the initial stimulus array. For instance, with an RA1-noun task some very low-functioning children might be presented initially with only a block and a stick of the same color in the stimulus array. Not until they could consistently make a differential response between these two objects were other objects introduced. The assistance thereby offered individual children could be both varied and subtle. Indeed, therein lay the beauty and power of this otherwise tedious and simple-minded procedure: It allowed for successive approximation to proceed in small enough steps, and by enough different routes, that it was practically always possible to maintain a high enough ratio of successful (reinforced) responses to unsuccessful (unreinforced) responses that a child did not become discouraged or unduly frustrated (ratio strain). In extreme cases, a 30 to 60 second "time out" followed incorrect responses (negative reinforcement).

While these general instructions pertained to all children and were explicit for each task, work with each child proceeded from an additional set of individually written instructions which were revised as frequently as necessary, often daily or even after each session.

Criterion. On 1- and 2-word tasks, the child was required to make 22 correct responses in a block of 25 trials in two consecutive sessions before he was given a post-test or moved on to a different task. This criterion had to be met with all nine objects present in the stimulus array and with all nine words being used as discriminative stimuli. The stipulation concerning two consecutive sessions was to permit a child to work with different adults in different sessions. When a child's performance with one adult deviates markedly from the performance on the same task with another adult, there is reason to suspect that there are unrecognized cues, possibly subtle, being displayed by one of the adults. The performances we were interested in were those which might be elicited by anybody, not those which only one person who has a "special knack" with a particular child might claim. For 3-word tasks, the criterion was 20 out of 25 responses correct in two consecutive sessions. Strictly prescribed post-tests were administered for most tasks, both to obtain a more standardized measure and to eliminate unrecognized non-random effects present during training. In these tests, the sequence of stimuli was randomized, no prompting or correction procedures were allowed, and there were no food reinforcers. In addition, on post-tests involving auditory stimuli, the adult sat behind the child so that visual cues such as subtle gestures or lip movements were unavailable. As the procedures evolved, pre-tests were sometimes administered to higher functioning children to determine whether some lengthy training sequences could be bypassed. If a child did not reach criterion with 1,050 training trials (14 sessions), he was considered not to have learned that task. In this case he would ordinarily switch to a task involving other receptive or expressive channels. However, with a few children who did not reach criterion even at the lowest task levels there seemed to be literally nowhere else to go, and training in the same tasks was sometimes continued beyond 14 sessions with additional variations.

The generalization tests were an attempt to infer whether a child could abstract from the 9WL objects with which he was familiar the qualities of "blockiness," "redness," etc. There were four separate generalization tests, each using different sets of objects, for receptive auditory, receptive visual, expressive speech, and expressive motor functions. In each case the generalization test consisted of 10 sets of the six relevant stimuli presented in random order. For example, in the receptive auditory generalization test the stimuli in each of the 10 sets would consist of the three adjectives and three nouns presented randomly. The first set was presented using the familiar 9WL objects. Each of the suceeding blocks of six trials used different sets of seven objects. These objects were chosen so as to be similar to one, and one only, of the nouns and adjectives. For example, a die or match box might be used instead of a block, a wire or pencil instead of a stick, a faucet washer or phonograph record instead of a ring. In addition, there was in each set a

FIG. 4. Objects used in generalization tests.

seventh object which was presumed to lack any qualities of either block, stick or ring, or of red, blue or yellow. Following the stimulus, the child would select an object from the array in front of him and place it in a flat box. A correct response was followed by the word "good" from the examiner and a morsel of food. The object was then placed back in the stimulus array before the next trial. When each new set of seven objects was presented, a child was allowed to examine or play with objects for 2 minutes, if he wished, before any stimuli were given. Once the first stimulus was presented, he no longer was permitted to play with any of the objects until that set of six trials was finished.

GENERAL CONSIDERATION OF RESULTS

Since perforce there were no control groups or individual matchings, each child needing to serve as his or her own control, it may seem unwarranted to draw general conclusions from the children studied. Yet, there were enough commonalities observed among the performances of individual children that a few summary statements about the forest may be helpful before moving closer to examine the trees. From the data on individuals to be presented in the following chapter, there appear to be some legitimate and fairly general inferences.

1. Autistic children can be systematically tested with the 9WL. There is no such thing as an untestable child. It is always possible to obtain consistent, predictable performance provided the tasks are made simple enough. Even the lowest functioning child in the series (*Charles*) displayed reliably measurable performance at the lowest level of testing for visual discrimination.

2. Children's responses on the 9WL showed all the properties of an operant, i.e., lawful relationships to discriminative and reinforcing stimuli which differed in no way from those relationships which are already well known. Some children already knew the basic nine words, and it remained only to rather quickly demonstrate the obvious (*Jonathan, Leon, Edgar, Orson, Curtis, Steve*). Where some or all of the basic nine words had to be learned, this was facilitated through the use of differential reinforcement, discriminative stimuli, temporary restriction of the stimulus array, and manipulation of reinforcement schedules (e.g., *Charles, Carl, Edward, Manuel, Stan*).

3. Lower functioning autistic children reached an impasse at some point on the 9WL grid. There appeared to be at least three types of impasses:

(a) Some children had *channel-specific deficits*, i.e., they conditioned readily to auditory stimuli but not to visual (*Carl, Stan*) or vice versa (*Andrew, Betsy, Leon*).

(b) Other children appeared to reach an impasse in relation to particular *parts of speech*. For example, *Stan*, who was very verbal but appeared clinically dyspraxic, was facile with nouns and adjectives but required extraordinary training to master verbs. *Carl*, mute but extremely dextrous and agile, mastered all three verbs in two sessions, while requiring 186 training sessions to reach criterion for nouns. *Manuel* and *Steve*, though not color blind, showed no difficulty in learning either nouns or verbs but had great difficulty learning adjectives.

(c) A third type of impasse was seen even in the absence of channel deficits or difficulties with particular parts of speech. This type appeared to involve a *limited "capacity"* to deal with compounded stimuli. To illustrate, some children knew all nine words perfectly, but if two of these words were put together they would display surprising difficulty in responding correctly to two familiar elements simultaneously. Adding a third word made it worse (e.g., *Manuel*). This was in contrast to most children who, once they learned words singly, could combine them in 2- and 3-word combinations without extra training. Some of these impasses were surmountable with extraordinary additional training; more commonly, it was not possible to elicit "higher" performance beyond these impasses even using training measures which tested the limits of our imaginations. This was commonest with channel-specific deficits.

4. Children who moved through the 9WL in minimum time and without impasses, when examined concerning higher language functioning, *also* displayed other impasses in such things as generalization and classification, cross-referencing, and syntactic transformations.

5. Each child was unique. This cliché takes on meaning when it is seen that each child generated a profile of linguistic abilities and disabilities which were special to him. Through highlighting certain similarities between children, subgroups may be tentatively suggested. One way to subgroup children would be according to the type of impasses described above. A broader conceptualization would divide those children who displayed serious difficulty of whatever sort in their basic conditionability of precision skills as detected by the 9WL from those children who displayed no such difficulty on the 9WL but reached other impasses at higher levels of language functioning.

6. A child's responding was ordinarily found to be patterned and stable, given a suitable reinforcement schedule, regardless of whether the task at hand had been mastered or not. In other words, stable, patterned responding was observed not only when a child had "learned" a task but also when he was "working at it" but still making many errors.

7. The most interesting information may be derived from a close scrutiny of stable error patterns. Thereby it often could be inferred that a child was operating according to a recognizable "strategy." His errors were not ordinarily random and chaotic. An autistic child, working comfortably within the confines of the 9WL, was not unpredictable and "out of contact." He was, as it were, experimenting with his world! And that can be observed on close scrutiny of almost any portion of the children's work which is presented in the following chapter.

8. Errors became less patterned and more random or "diffuse" at times, and seemed to signal one of two happenings: (a) increasing frustration, manifested by longer latencies, avoidance and tantrum behavior, and "giving up" (*Orson, Manuel*) or (b) as a prelude to task mastery (*Jonathan, Stan, Earl*). The former occurrence was simply a matter of poor training technique. In the latter case, it was as if an old theory or strategy were being given up and a new one taking its place.

9. Two characteristics of error patterns were rather general across children:

(a) Given a compound stimulus, i.e., one which contained two or more parts of speech, there was evident a sequence effect. The last word was responded to correctly, while the first word was often missed. For example, a child might know all adjectives and nouns of the 9WL. Given the stimulus "red block," he would respond consistently to *block* but erratically to *red*. Changing the stimulus to "block red" would result in his responding with consistent correctness to *red* and missing *block*. This sequence effect was ordinarily independent of the part of speech involved unless the child had displayed particular difficulty with particular parts of speech.

(b) Introduction of new words (even within the same part of speech) to a recently-mastered stimulus array often resulted in a loss of "old skills." For example, a child demonstrating 100% accuracy with a stimulus array which was limited to two objects would, upon introduction of a third object, begin making errors with all three objects, old and new alike (e.g., *Carl, Jonathan, Stan, Earl*).

10. Learning usually occurred rather suddenly, as if in all-or-none fashion. Newly learned tasks were then performed consistently, with short latencies and with accuracy approaching 100%.

Let us move closer to the trees.

CHAPTER 4

INDIVIDUAL CASE STUDIES

CHARLES

This boy, the son of a brilliant engineer, seemed oblivious to most environmental stimuli and often made no differential response between his parents and other people. He was diagnosed autistic and, furthermore, was the lowest functioning of the children tested with the 9WL. At the midpoint of 9WL work Charles was 6 years 8 months of age. He had 50 training sessions overall. Charles was mute except for infrequent guttural vocalizations. His Vineland Social Quotient was 23 and his Cattell-Binet IQ was 22. He was given a Social Rating of 5, indicative of profound withdrawal.

Charles was trained on 1-word tasks only, and stimuli were limited to nouns. In most sessions, nouns were limited to two objects of a single color. Despite this simplification and many additional cues, he never met criterion for either receptive auditory or receptive visual tasks. On post-test, where trials were randomized, his responses were at a chance level or below. Despite this failure to learn, close scrutiny of Charles' responding shows more than random behavior. There are response patterns or "strategies" which sometimes

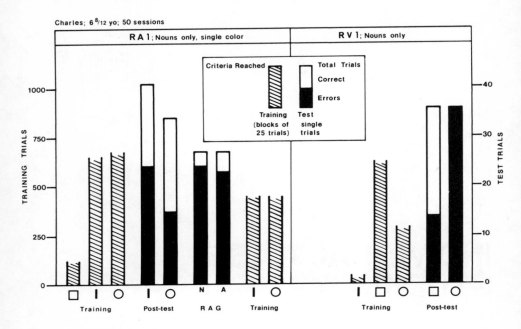

FIG. 5. Charles' histogram.

Legend: Cross-hatched bars represent training; each vertical unit = one block of 25 trials. Bars left open at top indicate criterion not reached. White and black bars represent test sessions; each vertical unit = one trial. Black portion = trial in which error made. □ = block; 1 = stick; O = ring.

lead to "success"; at other times, they drive his correct responses far below the chance level.

Under particular conditions of training, Charles displayed the following strategies at different times: perseveration (responding always to the same object); regular alternation between possible responses; repeating the last response if it had been reinforced or, if not reinforced, switching to a different response; responding to a particular stimulus dimension, ignoring other dimensions (e.g., on the receptive auditory generalization test, Charles displayed no awareness of shape dimension but showed a strong non-random response to the color dimension even though he had never been trained on colors and his color responses were incorrect); "obligatory" responses to novel stimuli when they were added to the stimulus array, even though such responses were never called for and never reinforced.

Certain things may be concluded about Charles' abilities and disabilities.

There is no doubt that he can make consistent visual discriminations between simple shapes. Also, his responses based on those visual discriminations can be shaped by means of differential reinforcement. Third, neither an auditory nor a visual discriminative stimulus appear to have any controlling effect on his responding. In other words, there is no evidence of auditory-visual or visual-visual associations. Thus, even though simple patterns of behavior can be shaped by their consequences, the fact that discriminative stimuli exert no controlling effect on Charles' behavior leaves these patterned responses of little adaptive consequence. He is like an archer who can regularly hit the mark provided some friend moves the target in front of his arrow.

ANDREW

Andrew was 6 years of age at the midpoint of training/testing with the 9WL. When diagnosed as an autistic child, his Vineland Social Quotient was 31, and his Cattell-Binet IQ score was 33. He was given a Social Rating of 5: He avoided interaction with others most of the time; sometimes he would accept lap-sitting, and at times he seemed aware of others, but was usually aloof and disinterested in both peers and adults. Often he would simply tantrum to signal his wishes, and when frustrated might either scratch people or engage in a flipping ritual. Follow-up at age 11 years, 3 months revealed that Andrew had only a few words of expressive speech, always used singly. He also used picture cards at times to communicate his wants, something he had been taught at the private residential school where he was at that time.

Andrew's case holds some special interest, for he was one of the first children with whom the 9WL was used. Previously, Andrew had been in the intensive operant training program (Hingtgen et al., 1967). At that time it had become apparent that he had a serious and clearly identifiable learning problem to which we had applied the term "cross-modal deficit." Although visual discrimination and visual memory were keen, Andrew demonstrated no ability to transfer auditory information to other sensory or expressive modalities. He could not connect what he heard with what he saw, or what he saw with sounds he uttered. After hundreds of hours of training during which we vainly tried to help Andrew get through or around this deficit, we largely abandoned auditory training and began to concentrate on Andrew's strength, i.e., his superior visual abilities. Our first intention was to present a manual sign language, similar to that used for communication among deaf people, with the idea that Andrew might learn either language or some practical signs for signaling wants. When this failed (for reasons explained below), we turned to the simpler and more systematic device of the 9WL to either train Andrew in manual communication or at least to better identify the reasons for failure. Since there had never been any evidence of ability to make auditory-visual associations, Andrew was trained only with the receptive visual and expressive motor portions of the 9WL. Training was discontinued before even this was completed due to a combination of slow progress and more pressing clinical considerations.

******

Training in "Manual Sign Language"

Recently there has been a renewal of interest in the possibilities of a manual sign language as a communication tool for autistic children who do not have functional speech (Benaroya, Wesley, Ogilvie, Klein & Meaney, 1977; Bonvillian & Nelson, 1976; Miller & Miller, 1973; Webster, McPherson, Sloman, Evans, & Kuchar, 1973). Our own effort with Andrew, who was one of very few children in whom we were unable to establish any functional speech whatsoever, was unsuccessful. Initially we had been optimistic because of Andrew's excellent visual memory, visual discrimination, and manual dexterity.

We began by training Andrew to make hand signs representing nine words: three nouns (baby, boy, girl), two adjectives (big, little), and four verbs (bathe, eat, drive, sleep). Our plan was to establish visual-hand sign associations and then to use these words in simple sentences. As it turned out, we did not get beyond trying to connect the three noun hand signs with their appropriate referents. Although Andrew quickly learned to associate one of three hand signs (baby, boy, girl) with dozens of stimulus objects, he appeared completely unable to generalize from the specific stimulus objects which were used in training to novel stimuli of the same class and objects. Dolls and pictures were used as the stimulus objects, and training consisted of the equivalent of 139 blocks of 25 trials, or 3,475 training trials. Although Andrew learned to respond correctly to all stimulus objects, testing Andrew with randomly presented novel stimuli (boys, girls, and babies) regularly resulted in no more than a chance level of correct response. It was as if the sign for each new boy, girl, or baby had to be learned afresh—as if the quality or concept of "boyness," "girlness," or "babyness" was not learned. To facilitate generalization, a certain amount of time was spent having Andrew sort the stimulus objects in one of three classes according to whether they represented a boy, girl, or baby. This he learned to do, and even showed some success in classifying novel pictures. Nevertheless, his association of hand signs to novel pictures never exceeded a chance level of success. On the final generalization test, following 80 hours of training, Andrew made correct hand signs in response to 81 of 99 familiar stimulus objects (82% correct) and then responded correctly to only 9 of 24 novel stimulus objects (37.5% correct).

Andrew also demonstrated a "strategy" in some sessions early in his training. He would rotate his responses in regular sequence, e.g., boy-girl-baby or girl-boy-baby, and stay within this pattern for the day. This resulted in his making the most correct responses to whichever stimulus occurred first in his particular pattern. A correction procedure, and eventually a time out procedure, was introduced to break up this stereotyped responding.

Believing that the stimulus objects might have a confusing degree of complexity and ambiguity, we elected to simplify and analyze our procedure rather than to expand it to the limit of Andrew's rote memory. We were still looking for syntax and language capability. Hence, the 9WL.

The 9WL was developed and operationalized as a result of our failure in teaching Andrew a useful sign language. We wanted to look at the problem in closer and more systematic detail. For this, we needed a system which would involve less ambiguous stimuli, permit precise recording of stimulus and response over a large series of trials, allow stepwise progression in complexity, be capable of rather formal description and analysis, be usable in obtaining information about various input and output channels, and possess the possibility of meaningful connection with both the phenomenology and deeper structure of everyday language.

Andrew was one of the children who were first exposed to the nine objects of the 9WL and with whom the establishment of procedures and criteria for task mastery were developed. This fact led to some difficulty in summarizing and analyzing his performance: Many of the training procedures were not so well established, and the early system of recording, we realized later, led to a loss of detail which precluded certain analyses. Therefore, the following material will focus on a few highlights without systematic, detailed analysis.

On the RV1 task, Andrew rather quickly learned to associate the three nouns with their signs and then encountered considerable difficulty before mastering the three adjectives. (On other tasks, Andrew had demonstrated good ability to discriminate colors.) He mastered these after 103 blocks of 25 trials (2,575 trials overall) and with some special restrictions of the stimulus array. He then rather quickly learned the three verbs, and on the RV1 post-test (which was only given after considerable RV2 training) he made only two errors in 50 randomized trials.

There followed a rather extended period of RV2 training (approximately 188 blocks of 25 trials) and of RV3 training (nine blocks of 25 trials) without Andrew's either reaching criterion or even showing much sign of progress.

After the initial unsuccessful efforts to train on RV2 and on RV3 tasks (and before the repeating of RV2 training in more systematic fashion), we turned to expressive motor tasks. (See Figure 6: EM1, EM2, EM3). From the outset, Andrew showed good ability to make the appropriate hand sign for either the color or the shape of the 9WL objects. He met criterion for EM1 training in minimum time and on a "post-test" made only one incorrect response in 76 trials. Immediately afterward, however, we were unable to train

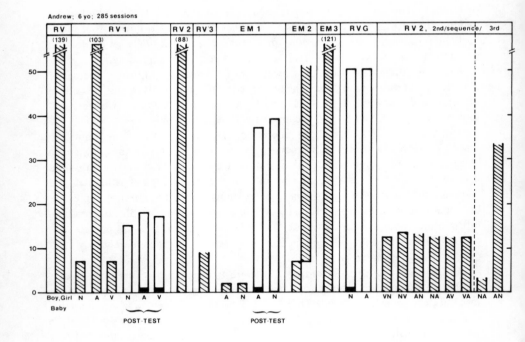

FIG. 6. Andrew's histogram. (For legend, see Figs. 2 and 5.)

Andrew to criterion on either EM2 or EM3 tasks. Our recording at the time precludes close scrutiny of possible reaons for this failure.

Andrew was then briefly returned to the RV1 task, culminating in 100 randomized RV1 trials in which he made 95 correct responses. He made three verb errors (all to the verb *give*), one adjective error, and one noun error. There were two "no response" trials. This seemed to confirm that he had mastered at least the RV1 task.

A receptive visual generalization test was then given consisting of 100 trials using all 9 words of the 9WL and 18 novel stimuli. (This test was different from the generalization tests which were lated used with other children in this series. The later tests employed fewer trials and a wider range of objects.) Andrew made 99 correct responses in 100 trials on this RVG, a result rather striking in view of his apparent inability to generalize when we were previously working with the manual sign language and the words boy, girl, and baby. This difference can probably be accounted for on the basis of the lesser ambiguity of the more recent stimuli and the greater amount of training with

Table 1. Andrew: Receptive Visual 2-Word Task (RV2), Second Training Sequence

	N/V	*V/N*	*N/A*	*A/N*	*V/A*	*A/V*
Errors out of 50 trials, successive sessions	22/1	18/1				
	29/1	13/0				
			31/4	29/0		
			32/3	29/4		
					15/8	35/1
					9/5	29/4
	38/8	27/2				
	18/6	34/2				
	32/0	8/1				
	7/4	4/0				
			25/5	23/0		
			25/2			
			30/1			
			26/6	24/0		
				23/0		
				29/0		
					14/0	14/0
					11/2	
					18/1	16/9
						21/9
						15/8

them. Thus, the earlier observation of Andrew's "inability to generalize" would appear to be relative to one or both of these factors.

At this point, our training procedure was further simplified and regularized and recording was done in more detail to permit a closer look at the lack of progress. We returned to the previously failed RV2 task. Andrew now did reach criterion on three of the six 2-word combinations in 12 to 14 blocks of 25 trials. On the other three 2-word combinations, he was not trained to criterion. Neither did he reach criterion 7 months later when exposed to this task a third time (see Fig. 6).

It now became apparent that Andrew's errors occurred mostly with respect to the first word of the 2-word stimulus. This is displayed in Table 1, and is referred to as a sequence effect. It was also apparent that Andrew experienced more difficulty in responding correctly to adjectives than to other parts of speech, regardless of the position of the adjective and the 2-word stimulus. Nevertheless, without exception he made many errors on the first element of the stimulus than on the second. This cannot be understood simply as a

Table 2. Andrew: Receptive Visual 2-Word Task (RV2), Third Training Sequence

	N/A	A/N
	14/0	
	13/0	
	12/0	
		11/1
		15/0
		12/0
		7/2
		9/1
		7/2
		13/0
		10/1
		11/1
		15/0
		15/0
		16/0
		12/0
		11/0
		10/0
		12/0
		12/0
		9/0
		8/0
		9/0
		14/0
		14/0
		10/0
		9/0
		10/0
		11/0
		14/0
		14/1
		9/1
		11/1
		14/0
		11/0

Errors out of 25 trials, successive sessions

matter of familiarity or proficiency with particular parts of speech. It would seem better to view this as a function of sheer time between stimulus and response (short term memory?) or as a function of intervening information which confounded Andrew's response, i.e., the second "bit" of information contained in the second word of the 2-word stimulus in some way interfered with his processing that "bit" of information contained in the first word of the 2-word stimulus, a kind of "stimulus competition." Perhaps Andrew could only integrate one "bit" at a time, either the ultimate or the penultimate stimulus, and beyond that exceeded his capacity. This interference notion would be supported by the observation that on those occasions when Andrew made an error on the ultimate stimulus he always responded correctly to the penultimate stimulus. But regardless of the explanation, it is exactly the error pattern observed in *Charles, Stanton*, and others. It might be thought of as a "linear" limitation in contrast to the two-way classification or "geometric" limitation of children such as *Leon* and *Jonathan*. The former limitation we have observed only in lower functioning autistic children, the latter only in higher functioning ones.

Another error pattern or strategy which was evident in Andrew's responding was his systematically rotating through all possible correct responses. This has been noted already in his initial work with the RV: boy-girl-baby task. Working on the RV2 task it reappeared. Thus, in response to the signed words "red stick," Andrew might respond consecutively with the yellow stick, then the blue stick, then the red stick. Asked next for, say, the blue block, he would again select the yellow and blue blocks in that sequence (or else begin with a red block, red being his last correct adjective response, then select the yellow block, and finally the blue block in that sequence.) By such a strategy, Andrew could regularly generate at least an FR3 schedule of reinforcement, sufficient it appeared to maintain stable responding but perhaps not conducive to further learning. This particular pattern was again successfully broken up by introducing a correction procedure and eventually a 30 second time out for incorrect responding.

At this time training with the 9WL was discontinued. We tried to use the information obtained therefrom to devise a program of more immediate practical value, including responding to cue cards and further auditory-vocal and visual-vocal training. Only 7 months later did we return to the RV2 task, exposing Andrew to more training sessions. (This was done to establish some baseline responding in preparation for an investigation of the effects of success and failure on autistic children.) Our experience again was that we could not train Andrew to criterion. At this point, however, virtually all of Andrew's errors appeared to be of a sequence effect type: In a noun-adjective sequence he made no adjective errors in 75 trials, but 39 noun errors! Reversing the sequence, he immediately eliminated noun errors but adjective errors now occurred on about half of the trials. Table 2 displays this pattern. Furthermore, trial-by-trial examination of the data again shows that on those occasions where the error occurs on the ultimate stimulus there is rarely an accompanying error on the penultimate stimulus.

CARL

Carl was mute except for infrequent vocalizations; he spoke no words. Neither was there ever a clear indication that he understood words. He was a small, very active and agile child who appeared to be unusually alert visually. At the midpoint of training/testing with the 9WL, Carl was 5 years of age. He had 256 training sessions overall. He had been diagnosed an autistic child and was given a Social Rating of 5 based on his extreme degree of withdrawal. A Cattell-Binet IQ of 35 was obtained, whereas an Adaptive Quotient of 62 was obtained.

Carl required extensive training on all receptive and expressive tasks. With rare exceptions to be noted, he reached criterion only when training was extended far beyond the usual cutoff point of 1,050 trials (14 sessions, 42 blocks of 25 trials). For example, on RV1 tasks he mastered nouns after 4,425 trials and adjectives after 2,775 trials. He did best on verbs, reaching criterion after only 650 trials. This performance was not matched on RA1 tasks, where he never reached criterion although he again demonstrated more facility in learning verbs than either nouns or adjectives. On tasks where he reached criterion in training sessions, he subsequently made few errors on post-tests; but when criterion had not been reached beforehand, his correct responses on post-tests were few. In other words, his records show either a chance level of correct responding or else nearly 100% correct responding. On generalization tests, Carl's correct responses were never significantly different from what would be expected by chance alone. He was neither trained nor tested with expressive speech tasks, since prior to his working on the 9WL he had been extensively trained to vocalize the words *shoe, man,* and *ball,* both repeating the spoken words (auditory-vocal association) and emitting the appropriate words in response to seeing the objects (visual-vocal association). His best speech production consisted of approximate vocalizations: "ōo," "bä," and "mä" for *shoe, ball,* and *man,* respectively. Although he could consistently vocalize approximations on hearing these words (auditory-vocal associations), he never achieved above the chance level in associating the sight of these three objects with his vocal productions (visual-vocal associations). Thus, it may be inferred that Carl would have displayed at least as much difficulty with ES1 tasks as he did with RA1, RV1, and EM1 tasks.

This child's difficulty in learning the RA1 tasks may be further appreciated when it is realized that the stimulus array was severely restricted throughout

Carl; 5 yo; 256 sessions

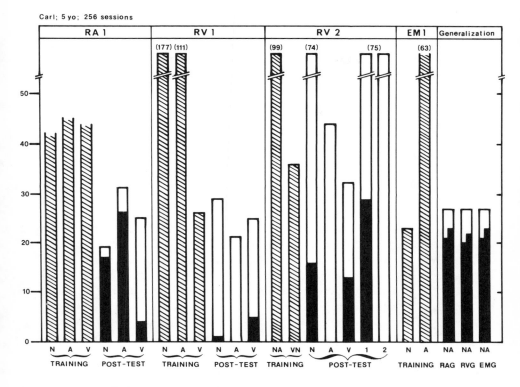

FIG. 7. Carl's histogram. (For legend, see Figs. 2 and 5.)

both noun and adjective training. While working on nouns, the stimulus array was limited to three objects of one color only. While working with adjectives, the stimulus array was limited to three colors of one shape only. Moreover, during the first four-fifths of his training with adjectives, only *red* and *blue* were given as discriminative stimuli (never *yellow*). Despite this, he continued to make "yellow" responses ($\overline{Y}$ = 6.8 + 1.6 X per 25 trials) with no evidence of extinction. Once *yellow* was included among the discriminative stimuli, with consequent reinforcing of correct "yellow" responses, these responses increased significantly to 9.1 ± 1.6 X per 25 trials ($p < .001$, t test, two-tail), although his correct responses to a *yellow* discriminative stimulus remained at a chance level. Thus, as with *Charles*, it is apparent that his responses were partially controlled by differential reinforcement but were not controlled by discriminative stimuli.[6]

It is of some interest that Carl learned verbs more readily than either nouns or adjectives on the RA1 tasks; this greater proficiency with verbs is reflected in his RA1 post-test. As noted, this child's agility and grace in moving through space—particularly when contrasted with the clumsiness and apparent dyspraxia of *Stan*, a child who had much more difficulty in mastering verbs than other parts of speech—makes this relative facility with verbs especially intriguing.

Looking more closely at Carl's work with RA1 verbs, we see that when limited to the verbs *give* and *tap*, he suddenly met criterion after 26 blocks of 25 trials and then made only one error on each of 4 consecutive blocks. However, when the third verb (*slide*) was introduced, he began making more errors, not only on *slide* but also on the previously mastered *give* and *tap*. Limiting the stimulus array to a single object resulted in his making only four to seven errors per 25 trials. Although this did not meet the high criterion of the 9WL, his relatively good performance with verbs was maintained on the post-test, where all nine objects were present and all nine words randomly presented as discriminative stimuli. The five verb errors were all in response to *slide*, and in four of these instances there was at least a "verb" response to the *verb* cue. It is also noted on this post-test that on 21 occasions he added a "verb" response to a noun or adjective discriminative stimulus, which, in 11 cases, vitiated an otherwise correct response. Aside from the obvious bearing this had on Carl's learning (i.e., receiving negative feedback in relation to a partially correct response), it also indicates that he was overusing a class of responses with which he had previously had most success. This might be viewed simply as a consequence of differential reinforcement (more verb responses had been reinforced) or of sequence of training (most recently trained on verbs). In any event, the fact remains that although he usually responded correctly to a verb discriminative stimulus, he also overgeneralized these verb responses so that irrelevant discriminative stimuli (noun and adjective) elicited these verb responses as well.

Carl had training on RV1 tasks on two separate occasions, with EM1 training in between. Initially, there were 48 training sessions (sessions 50–97)

---

[6]This phenomenon of behavior, which is controlled by consequences but not by antecedents, may be highly significant in understanding the deviant behavior of perceptually handicapped children: Some responses become very strongly established, but they never come under control of discriminative stimuli, which is a technical way of saying that they never help the child adapt to or cope with his world. Many responses are established and maintained by their occasional reinforcing consequences, but only when such responses are also controlled by pertinent discriminative stimuli will the behavior be what we call "appropriate."

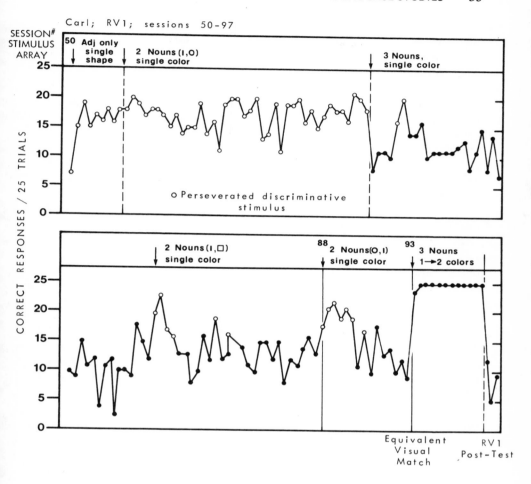

FIG. 8. Carl: Receptive Visual 1-word task (RV1), sessions 50–97.

with criterion not being reached on any part of speech. It is noted that higher than chance levels of correct responses occurred only under special circumstances such as perseverating the discriminative stimulus, severely restricting the array of stimulus objects, or giving additional prompts which rather force a correct response. It is also noteworthy that in session 93, rather than using a hand sign for the discriminative stimulus, an identical object was presented as the discriminative stimulus, i.e., the task was switched to one of equivalent visual matching. Instantly, Carl learned this task, making only one error in 12 blocks (300 trials)! A post-test, using nouns only, but reverting to the usual hand signs, resulted in his correct responses again being near the chance level.

In a second, more extended sequence of RV1 training (sessions 145–209), Carl did show further learning. This seemed to occur through restricting both the discriminative stimuli and the array of stimulus objects. Several things are noteworthy. First, when learning occurred, as measured by the number of correct responses, it occurred rather quickly, usually within one or two sessions. Carl's correct responding then remained at a high level—so long as no additional elements were added to the task! However, if a new element be added, his correct responses are likely to drop at once. For example, after considerable training on adjectives only (20 sessions, 1,500 training trials), using a single shape in the array of stimulus objects (three objects in all), Carl rather suddenly eliminated practically all errors. (See Figure 9, sessions 181–183.) Having "learned" the task at this level of complexity, in session 184 objects of two shapes were included in the stimulus array, now six objects in all. Although the discriminative stimuli continued to be only those adjectives which he had been working with for the previous 23 sessions, his correct responses immediately dropped to a chance level, and correct responding to adjectives was not securely reestablished for another 5 sessions. Once he accomplished this, he did not become similarly discombobulated when, in session 192, a third shape was added (now a full array of nine stimulus objects). The same phenomenon was observed, however, following session 196 when Carl began working on verbs alone. Although he mastered this task much more quickly than he did adjectives, it was again seen, in session 200, that when a full array of stimulus objects was introduced his correct responses immediately dropped. However, his recovery in this case was much swifter. Beginning with session 204, Carl was trained using a full complement of nine discriminative stimuli and nine objects in the stimulus array, showing progressive improvement. Finally, the RV1 post-test displayed a high and rather consistent level of correct responses.

Carl's performance on the RVG test was almost identical to his previous performance on the RAG test. In both cases, there was no evidence of his ability to generalize correct responding beyond the specific stimulus objects with which he had been trained.

It was clear, despite the vicissitudes of RV1 training detailed above, that Carl had learned to make consistently correct responses to each of the nine words when presented one at a time. The next question was whether he could also handle two words at a time. On RV2 tasks, Carl was trained with only two sequences of words: *noun* plus *adjective*, and *verb* plus *noun*. Most of his training was on the former. From the histogram it is seen that he reached criterion on both of these tasks, although extended training was again required

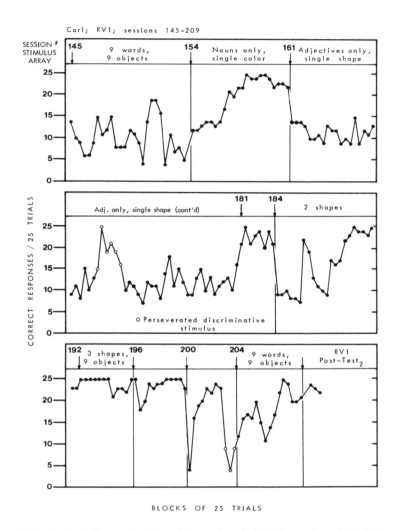

FIG. 9. Carl: Receptive Visual 1-word task (RV1), sessions 145–209.

Table 3. Carl: Receptive Visual 2-Word Task (RV2) Errors in Blocks of 25 Trials

Session	N_1	A_2	Session	N_1	A_2	Session	N_1	A_2
210	12	2	220	6	1	230	7	0
	8	4		2	0		9	0
	1	2		2	0		11	0
	9	8		6	0	231	16	0
	10	11		4	0		10	0
	8	8		2	0		9	0
212	12	0		12	0	232	9	0
	7	0		12	0		9	0
	11	0		12	1		16	0
213	10	2		13	1	233	11	0
	10	2		10	5		11	0
	9	4		15	0		11	1
214	7	4		8	0	234	12	0
	11	4		9	0		13	0
	11	4		11	0		10	2
215	8	2		15	1		12	0
	9	5		14	1		12	0
	11	0		11	1		15	0
	11	0		10	0		15	0
	11	0		12	1			
	10	0		11	1			
	3	0		2	0			
	7	0		6	1			
	2	0		5	0			
	9	0		11	0			
	12	0		16	0			
	7	0		12	0			
219	12	0		12	2			
	7	0		10	1			
	5	0		19	1			

Table 3. (cont'd)

Session	V_1	N_2	Session	V_1	N_2
236	10	4	246	8	0
	6	5		7	0
	2	5		6	0
	1	6		6	0
	4	3		7	0
	7	1		8	0
	7	3		13	2
	10	1		11	0
	11	0		10	0
	11	5		5	5
	9	4		11	0
	13	4		8	0
	8	1		7	0
	9	0		7	0
	10	2		9	0
	12	4		5	0
	12	5		9	0
	19	2		5	0
	6	1		10	0
	10	0		3	0
	11	0		9	0
243	9	3		4	1
	9	4		4	0
	10	1		8	0
	5	0		8	1
	7	0		9	3
	7	0		8	1
245	5	2	255	10	0
	10	1		8	0
	9	0		6	0

N = noun; A = adjective; V = verb. Subscripts 1 and 2 indicate first and second elements of 2-word stimulus.

Table 4. Carl: Receptive Visual 2-Word Task (RV2)

Session	Trial	S^D	Response	Session	Trial	S^D	Response
210	4	□Y	1Y	213	43	OR	1R
	5	□Y	□B		44	OR	□R
	45	OY	1Y		45	OR	1R
	46	OY	OR		46	OR	□R
211	7	□R	1R		47	OR	OR-P
	8	□R	□Y		48	OR	OR
	14	OB	OY		49	OR	OR
	15	OB	□B		53	OB	1B
	16	OB	OY		54	OB	OR
	17	OB	□B		55	OB	□B
	20	OR	OY		56	OB	□B
	21	OR	□Y		57	OB	OR
	22	OR	□B		58	OB	OB
	23	OR	1R	214	62	1Y	□Y
	24	OR	OR-P		63	1Y	1B
	25	OR	OR		64	1Y	1Y
	38	OB	1B		65	OR	OY
	39	OB	1R		66	OR	1R
	40	OB	□R		67	OR	OR
	41	OB	OR		68	1R	OR
	42	OB	OY		69	1R	1R
	43	OB	OB		73	OY	1Y
213	19	OY	1Y		74	OY	OB
	20	OY	OR		75	OY	1Y
	21	OY	OY		76	OY	OY

□ = block; O = ring; 1 = stick; B = blue; Y = yellow; R = red; -P = prompted response.

for him to reach this level of performance on the *noun* plus *adjective* (NA) task (2,475 trials). Detailed inspection of his records reveals new kinds of errors and suggests some of the strategies employed by Carl in mastering this newly complicated task.

The most salient feature is a strong sequence effect: Almost all errors are made in relation to the first element of the discriminative stimulus regardless of which part of speech occupies this position. In other words, if the stimulus is noun plus adjective, Carl misses nouns; if it is verb plus noun, he misses verbs. His errors in relation to the second (proximate) element of the discriminative stimulus are rare, and there is no statistically significant difference as to which part of speech occupies this position. This strong sequence effect continues not only through his training to criterion but is also evident on the RV2 post-test. There he makes some noun and verb errors but only when they are presented as the first element of the discriminative stimulus. He makes no errors on the proximate element regardless of the part of speech involved.

Examining Carl's record trial by trial suggests how he goes about solving his problem. Some excerpts of raw data will be used to demonstrate (see Table 4). In Carl's first RV2 training session (number 210) he is seen to exchange one error for another. For example, the stimulus (via hand signs, remember) is *block yellow*. He responds "stick" "yellow," which is not correct. He is not reinforced, and the discriminative stimulus, *block yellow*, is repeated. He now responds "block" "blue." He has corrected his error on the first element of the discriminative stimulus but at the same time has switched his response to the second element from a correct to an incorrect one. This pattern recurs. Indeed, on those rare occasions when he responds incorrectly to the proximate element of a discriminative stimulus, it usually occurs on a trial in which he is correcting a previous error in relation to the first element of the same discriminative stimulus. This can also be expressed statistically, since we find that an error occurring on the second element has a higher than chance probability of being associated with a correct response to the first element (χ^2 = 69.3, $p < .001$).[7] This type of difficulty, as demonstrated on the RV2 task, points to an important problem for Carl in handling *linguistic structure* even beyond the important problem of *basic conditionability* which was demonstrated in the RV1 tasks. Thus, he appears to have two different kinds of impairment.

As Carl proceeds it is noted that, despite continuing errors, his responses are not just random. He displays a systematic search, suggesting some strategy. For instance, in session 211, trials 20 through 25, he seems to be fixing half of his response, while experimenting with the other half. This could be seen as a more sophisticated trial-and-error type of search, but still he is not "using"

---

[7]The implications of this type of error for normal language development are extraordinary. It is as if all stimuli are perceived as simple, containing only one element, only one "bit" of information. Logically, the task is that of perceiving a complex stimulus as containing two or more bits of information and appreciating that (a) each bit has a fixed value or meaning and that (b) each bit can vary in relation to other bits without changing its own value or meaning. This error of "monolithism" is found entrenched not only in extremely low-functioning autistic children such as Carl, but also in fully verbal ones. Compare, for instance, *Leon's* inability to integrate prepositions into functional speech: The preposition "beside" is regularly associated with the noun "cup" as if *beside cup* contained only one bit of information rather than two. The effect of a persistent error of this type on the language development of either child can only be devastating.

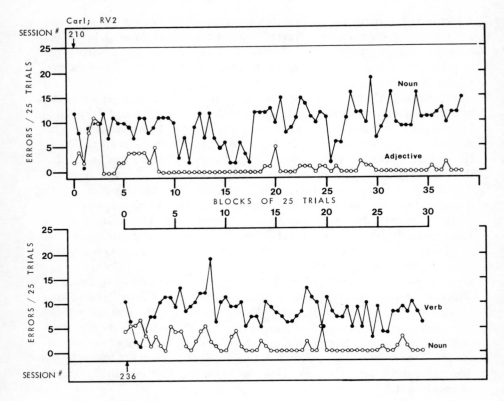

FIG. 10. Carl: Receptive Visual 2-word task (RV2).

the information available to him in the discriminative stimulus. This is evident again in trials 39 through 43 where, in response to *ring blue*, he fixes first his adjective response (in this case, "red") while rotating systematically through all noun possibilities, and then fixes his noun response ("ring") while rotating systematically through all adjective possibilities until finally arriving at the correct response—which is reinforced!

Looking at the data more broadly, it appears that Carl is experimenting with various strategies through the first five or six of the RV2 training sessions for noun plus adjective. During *these* sessions, his errors occur in relation to both first and second stimulus elements, back and forth. He then settles into a rather stable pattern of responding correctly to almost all second elements and making virtually all of his errors on the first elements of the discriminative stimuli. Couched in motivational terms, we might speculate that he has found the best available solution. This pattern is repeated with the verb plus noun sequence. (See Figure 10.)

It thus appears that a study of Carl's error patterns may be most revealing shortly after he begins a new task and is actively trying to solve some new problems; subsequently, his response pattern may stablize in some fashion which yields an acceptable schedule of reinforcement, i.e., sufficient to maintain responding. But the search has been abandoned, and new learning is not to be expected unless conditions are again changed. One could be tempted to surmise that much of an autistic child's meeting—or failing to meet—the world follows such a pattern.

The end of Carl's experience with the 9WL consisted of an RV2 post-test in which, regardless of part of speech, he made only first element errors.

Carl had 40 training sessions on EM1 tasks sandwiched between the two spates of RV2 training. He was trained first on nouns only, reaching criterion in 23 blocks. Not only did he fail to reach criterion on adjectives in 21 sessions (1,575 trials), but he also showed no improvement despite the fact that the array of stimulus objects was limited to sticks only and despite his being given numerous additional cues to facilitate learning. His having more difficulty with adjectives than with nouns is understandable perhaps since the relevant stimulus dimensions may be considered more abstract. We have already seen that Carl displayed no ability to abstract, at least in the sense of generalizing beyond the specific objects with which he had been trained. Another relevant factor might be that the hand signs for adjectives are not as suggestive of a correct response as the hand signs for nouns may be. In any case, his difficulty in mastering the EM1 task is all the more remarkable in the context of his having completed just previously over 50 sessions on RV1 tasks in which he was required to imitate a single hand sign before he selected the corresponding object. It must be noted, however, that he had not at that point reached criterion on RV1. Possibly, had EM1 tasks been repeated after his second period of training on RV1, when he had in fact reached criterion, he might have more quickly demonstrated ability to give the noun or adjective sign for an object upon seeing it. But, this was not done, and no more can be said about his EM1 performance. No EM1 post-test was given, and the series was concluded with an EMG test. The numerical results were identical to his RA and RV generalization tests: a chance level of correct responding. Trial-by-trial inspection reveals a perseverated "ring" response (36 of 54 responses) which produced 6 of his 10 correct responses overall—produced them, as it were, by collision with the randomly occurring *ring* discriminative stimulus. So again in the face of a baffling task, Carl settled on a kind of rigidity of response.

STAN

Stan was a relatively high-functioning autistic child. He was 7 years of age at the midpoint of his work with the 9WL. He had 98 training/testing sessions over a period of 3 months. At the time of diagnosis, his Vineland Social Quotient was 42. His IQ on the Peabody Picture Vocabulary was 36, while on the Stanford-Binet test it was 37. He was given a Social Rating of 4, reflecting rather pervasive withdrawal with occasional more personal or affectionate responses to people he knew well. There is no follow-up information.

Stan was a large, clumsy, red-haired child who had a great deal of very clear speech. Most of it was echolalic. He was an anxious and irritable child, becoming acutely distressed when asked to do anything. An invitation to play ball would result in a tantrum. Insisting that he play ball disclosed not just poor coordination but seeming unawareness of what to do. Left to himself, he would spend many hours flipping wire or bits of string. There was no appropriate toy play. In simple adaptive skills such as dressing himself, washing his hands, or helping to set the table, Stan seemed once again to be

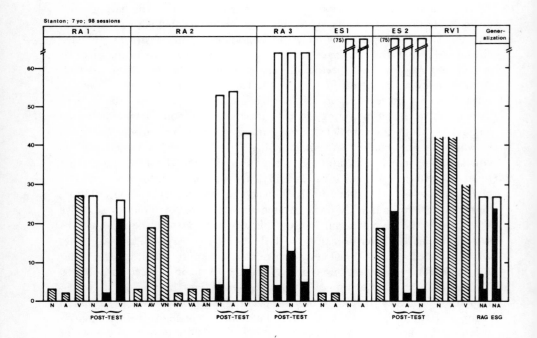

FIG. 11. Stan's histogram. (For legend, see Figs. 2 and 5.)

Stan; RA1; Verbs

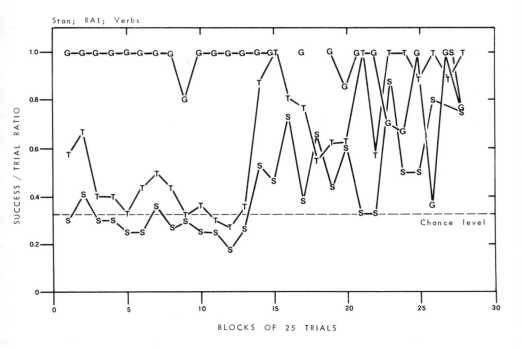

FIG. 12. Stan: Receptive Auditory 1-word task (RA1), verbs.

at a loss, not knowing what to do. He needed to be instructed or directed each step of the way. He ignored peers except to occasionally bully smaller children. He seemed to find pleasure in taking things from them and pinching or kicking them.

Beginning with the RA1 task, Stan demonstrated competence with nouns and adjectives immediately. This was scarcely a surprise, because he was a highly verbal child. What did cause surprise was that verbs were by no means easy for him. He required training for 27 blocks (675 trials) before reaching criterion on the 3 verbs. That he should have especial difficulty learning only the verb tasks is of particular interest in view of the clinical observation of dyspraxia. This child, who clinically seemed unable to program himself to throw a ball or put on his pants, was now having trouble in responding to three simple verbs. Looking at this in more detail, we see that he initially made errors in response to the verbs *tap* and *slide*; for the first 200 trials he made no errors in response to *give*. One remarkable feature is that as he began to improve his success/failure ratio in response to *tap* and *slide*, he began making errors in response to *give* (Fig. 12). It is reasonable to assume that through-out his life Stan had had much more exposure to the verb *give* than to either *tap* or *slide*. Thus, it is not surprising that this is the one verb to which he always responds correctly. What is of interest is that his performance in response to *give* deteriorates as his performance in response to the relatively unfamiliar verbs, *tap* and *slide*, improves. Again, this seems to be an example of a diffusion of an old error pattern which occurs prior to the integration of some new skills. (A similar phenomenon has already been described for *Carl*.) By the time Stan reached criterion for all three verbs together, his errors were few and were rather evenly distributed across all three verbs. That he continued to have greater difficulty with verbs than with nouns or adjectives, however, is seen on the RA1 post-test where, in 75 randomized trials, 21 of his 23 errors are in response to verbs (*slide* and *tap* only, never *give*). Therefore we may conclude that although Stan was not incapable of learning correct responses to verb forms, they presented special difficulties for him; and we were especially intrigued by the possible relation between this disability and his clinically apparent dyspraxia.

Stan's next training was on the ES1 task. Presented with one of the nine stimulus objects, he was to say the appropriate noun, adjective, or both (visual-vocal association). He met criterion in minimum time and made no errors on a post-test consisting of 75 randomized trials.

Stan worked next on RA2 tasks. He had no trouble with noun + adjective (NA) combinations, but when he moved to adjective + verb combinations (AV) he did not reach criterion until 19 blocks of training (475 trials) because of lingering difficulty with verbs. The error pattern is very similar to that seen on the RA1 task (see Figure 13, first portion) except that Stan moved more quickly to mastery. He next moved to verb + noun (VN) combinations. Here, he maintained almost flawless performance on verbs, but he suddenly started making errors on nouns. This is astounding. He knew nouns from the beginning, and previous errors on nouns are hard to find; now he is finally responding to verbs with consistent correctness and is missing many nouns! The sequence effect, evident in so many other children on RA2 and RV2 tasks, is not seen here, i.e., he is responding correctly to the first element of the discriminative stimulus and missing the second. (See Figure 14, especially session 27.)

Once again, closer scrutiny of the data yields further information and suggests an explanation. On beginning the verb + noun task in session 27, Stan's first block of trials resulted in seven verb errors and no noun errors ("sequence effect"). But the next 25 trials in the same session resulted in only one verb error while for the first time he makes errors on nouns. It is as if for only a moment he has lost and recovered his recently acquired skill with verbs—but at the expense of losing even longer-held mastery of nouns (Figs. 13 & 14). This

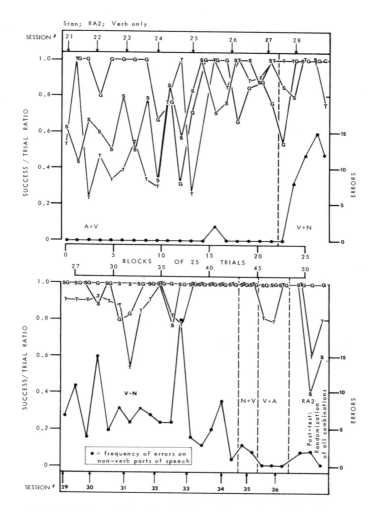

FIG. 13. Stan: Receptive Auditory 2-word task (RA2), verbs only.

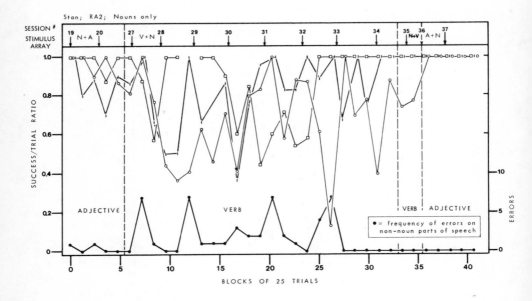

FIG. 14. Stan: Receptive Auditory 2-word task (RA2), nouns only.

pattern of getting verbs correct and missing nouns continues for another 20 blocks (500 training trials) before Stan reaches criterion. In session 34, when the sequence is reversed from verb + noun to noun + verb, he does not stumble. Finally, verbs + adjectives and adjectives + nouns present no difficulties. On the RA2 post-test, in which parts of speech are independently randomized across the first and second elements of the discriminative stimulus for 75 trials, in responding to 150 discrete stimulus elements, Stan made only 12 errors—5 on the first element of the discriminative stimulus, 7 on the second. Of these 12 errors, the first 4 were all on nouns and the last 8 were all on verbs.

On the RAG test, Stan generalized accurately on 46 of 54 novel stimuli, making 6 noun and 2 adjective errors. This seems to fit the pattern of most children on generalization tests, namely, that noun errors predominate over adjective errors.

Stan next had eight sessions on the ES2 task in which he observed the adult performing one of the three 9WL actions using any one of the nine stimulus objects. The task was for Stan to say the appropriate verb and either the color or shape of the object, or both. A correct response therefore consisted in either two or three words, one of which had to be a verb and all

Table 5. Stan: Sessions 43 and 82.

	Task: ES2 Session 43			Task: RV1-Adj Session 82	
Trial	S^D	Response	Trial	S^D	Response
26	TYO	YO	16	Y	Y1
27	TYO	SYO	17	R	Y□
28	TYO	S O	18	R	R□(P)
29	TYO	T O	19	R	R□
30	SB□	S □	20	B	R□
31	SR1	S 1	21	B	BO(P)
32	TYO	S O	22	B	B1
33	TYO	SY	23	Y	B□
34	TYO	T O	24	Y	Y1(P)
35	TBO	BO	25	Y	Y□
36	TBO	SBO			
37	TBO	T O			
38	TY1	TYO			
39	TY1	TY			
40	TY□	Y□			
41	TY□	S □			
42	TY□	T □			

Legend: T = tap; S = slide; Y = yellow; B = blue; R = red; □ = block; O = ring; 1 = stick; *(P)* = prompted correct response.

of which had to be correct. In Stan's first block of 25 trials, he made 20 errors. Sixteen of these were failure to say the verb; on three occasions he spoke an incorrect verb. By his second block of 25 trials, he seemed to have established the proper "set" in that there were only three verb omissions. However, his successes were not increased, because he persistently said the wrong verb. During this time he experimented with altering his noun and adjective responses while tending to perseverate the verb *slide*. As training progressed, his errors on verbs decreased. At the same time, errors with nouns and adjectives appeared. He reached criterion after 19 blocks, at which time his remaining errors were predominantly with verbs. On a post-test of 75 trials, he responded correctly 49 times. He made only one erroneous verb response, two erroneous adjective responses, and three erroneous noun responses. Twenty-two errors were scored for failure to respond with the verb component of the stimulus.

On the expressive speech generalization test (ESG), Stan then made only 29 correct responses to 54 novel stimuli. As in his ES2 post-test, his poor performance may be related to his losing the proper "set." Ten errors were scored because he accurately named an object ("screwdriver," "solder spool") or the object with which the stimulus might be associated ("car," in response to a toy tire). On ten occasions he named the "wrong" part of speech, e.g., "orange" in response to an orange *block*. On three occasions he made seemingly irrelevant responses, and on another three no response.

Stan next worked for five sessions on RA3. The first and last sessions were a pre- and post-test, respectively. Unfortunately, the sequence of parts of speech was different in the training sessions and testing sessions so that interpretation of results is confounded. This may account for his better performance on pre-test than on post-test. However, Stan quickly reached criterion in training sessions. He displayed practically no errors on verbs, regardless of their place in the 3-word sequence; about two-thirds of his errors were on nouns.

The last task on which Stan was trained was the RV1 task. He had 14 training sessions each on nouns and adjectives. Not only did he not reach criterion with either part of speech, but he demonstrated no progress on either task despite restrictions of the stimulus array and additional cues. Throughout, he usually made between 25 and 35 correct responses in 75 trials. Occasional higher scores occurred only because of stimulus persevera-tion. By prearrangement, training on these two parts of speech was discontinued after 14 sessions. He had had only 10 training sessions on RV1-verbs when work with the 9WL was discontinued because of independent clinical considerations. At the time of discontinuation, Stan was showing some progress with verbs (using a restricted stimulus array), averaging 58 correct responses across his last 3 sessions. Criterion was not reached.

Stan's better performance with verbs than nouns or adjectives on the RV1 task might be due to growing exposure to the general pattern of the RV1 task. Also, it might be argued that the verb hand signs more strongly suggest their referents than do the adjective or even noun hand signs. But the most striking comparison is between Stan's noun and adjective performance, RA1 vs. RV1. He had not the slightest trouble in mastering the auditory version of this task, while visually he made no progress in 2,250 trials. It is reasonable to assume that visual perception or visual-motor integrations posed a stumbling block here. Since, in other contexts, he showed adequate visual perception to the point of being able to "read" some words (i.e., word call), it seems more reasonable to implicate problems with visual-motor integration. This conclusion is supported by the observation that Stan had great difficulty in imitating the hand signs which were given as discriminative stimuli for RV1 tasks, something he was required to do before he was allowed to respond by selecting an object.

Behavioral notes from sessions suggest a strong association between Stan's success level and particular types of behavior. When responding with a high rate of success, he was generally attentive and cooperative. When having difficulty, there were many reports of his being preoccupied, inattentive, cursing, flailing his arms, and at times trying to hit, kick, or bite the adult. Nowhere is this more striking than with the RV1 tasks, and particularly when adults were insisting that he imitate the hand sign before responding. Once again we are reminded of his dyspraxia and must suspect its effect on his poor learning of this task. We might wonder, if the intermediate step of imitating the hand sign were omitted, whether he might be better able to encode for a direct nonequivalent visual-visual match (particular hand signs matched to particular objects). Indeed, his *initial* response to the hand signs was to make only a vocal response followed by placing an object in the box. But learning in this way was not investigated further.

Trial-by-trial examination of his records indicates that despite lack of progress on RV1, Stan nevertheless adopted certain strategies at various times. There was the common one of perseverating his last success. (See Table 5, RV1 task.) Another strategy became apparent on adjective training when, for a period, he associated color hand signs with object shapes. For instance, in response to the *yellow* hand sign, Stan would say stick; after *blue*, he would say block. The red hand sign would be followed by his looking in the box and naming any object which was not present there.

Despite the inconclusiveness on this point, we are left with suggestive evidence overall that Stan encountered at least two types of impasses on the 9WL: (1) parts of speech (verbs) and (2) channel-specific (visual or visual-motor). It is possible that when clinically appeared to be dyspraxia was common to both of these learning problems.

LEON

Leon was 6 years of age at the midpoint of his 9WL work. When diagnosed as an autistic child, his Vineland Social Quotient was 77. His Peabody Picture Vocabulary IQ was 62, while on the Cattell-Binet his IQ was 44. His Social Rating was 4, indicating only occasional personal contact with familiar people. There is no follow-up information.

Leon was a robust and active child who, against a background of general withdrawal, would move abruptly and make momentary contacts with people and things. Similarily, his speech, which was usually a quiet autistic reverie, would occasionally explode in a loud outburst. There was virtually no sustained relating to either children or adults. Most of the echolalic utterances seemed to be delayed reproductions of what he had heard on TV or phrases from home. On the ward it was noted that he would not ask for things for himself (even though showing interest) until after he had just heard another child ask; *then* Leon would ask. Similarly, in music therapy he seemed never to use either the melody or the lyrics to guide himself in "action songs"; rather, he would watch his peers and imitate their behavior, thus always remaining behind the music. Hence it appeared that Leon's speech was limited to rote memory and that he was somewhat better able to use visual than auditory information.

Work with Basic 9WL

As shown in the histogram, Leon reached criterion on all 9WL tasks with little or no training. On receptive auditory tasks, his performance was practically errorless up to the point of pre-testing on the RA3 task. Here, many errors suddenly appeared, principally related to the emergence of a

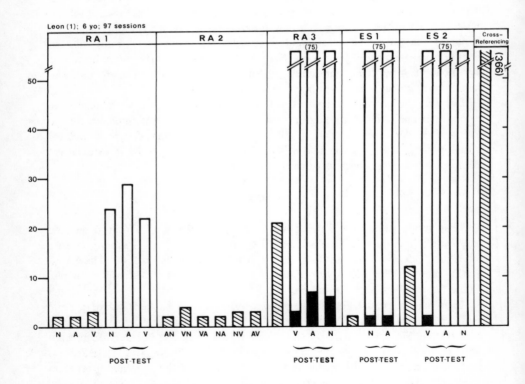

FIG. 15. Leon's histogram (1). (For legend, see Figs. 2 and 5.)

stereotyped "give" response to the verb element. After being trained for 21 blocks of 25 trials on the RA3 task, he satisfactorily passed the RA3 post-test.

On the ES1 task, Leon again required minimal training and on post-test made only 4 errors in 75 trials. Somewhat more training was required before Leon reached criterion on the ES2 task, since he had some difficulty in reporting the demonstrated verb. Although he reached criterion in 12 training blocks and made only 2 errors on the post-test, his operational strategy (superstitions?), which still provided continuous reinforcements on the ES2 task, is of interest: If the verb *give* were demonstrated, his response would be correct and consist of verb, adjective, noun, in that sequence; however, if either *tap* or *slide* were demonstrated, his response would again be correct but would consist of the appropriate adjective followed by the appropriate verb. If he deviated from this pattern, he would be likely to make an error.

When moving to receptive visual tasks, Leon once more had very little difficulty. This is again demonstrated by the low profile histogram. Not until reaching the RV3 task was additional training necessary to reach criterion (19 blocks, 475 trials). He then made only 10 errors on the post-test, 9 of them being in relation to the first element of the three-part (adjective-noun-verb) stimulus. Since he had previously displayed no difficulty with adjectives on any RV task, these errors probably represent a sequence effect.

Within 6 blocks of 25 trials, Leon had met criterion on the EM1 task. Before Leon added the verb to the EM2 responses, he had been trained for an additional 34 blocks. Once criterion was reached, he made only four errors on the post-test. By this time, he displayed the same strategy and error pattern as he had on the ES2 task, namely, making the signs for verb, adjective, noun in that sequence when the stimulus included the verb *give*, and making the signs for adjective + verb when the stimulus included the verbs *slide* or *tap*.

On all four generalization tests, Leon clearly showed good ability to generalize beyond the specific stimuli with which he had been previously trained. The numbers alone are convincing, and examinations of trials in which errors were scored indicates even more strongly that Leon was well able to grasp these tasks. On the RVG task, three of his errors might be considered "near misses." For instance, he responded to *red* by selecting an orange object. His other three errors on RVG were ones which he corrected spontaneously, although they were still scored as errors. Similarly, on the EMG task, all of his errors were scored for failure to make any hand sign response, although in each case he made the correct verbal response. On ESG, he again corrected himself on four of his six errors.

Overall, then, Leon had clearly demonstrated his competence with the 9WL. His receptive auditory and visual channels and his expressive vocal and motor channels were adequate to reliably deal with at least three words (and

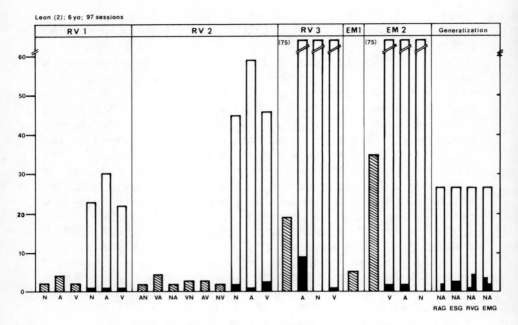

FIG. 16. Leon's histogram (2). (For legend, see Figs. 2 and 5.)

parts of speech) at a time. In addition, he had demonstrated through each modality the ability to abstract or generalize his training and to apply it in new situations. With Leon's fundamental competence in conditionable tasks established, we moved to train and examine him in more functional speech. Our efforts were divided into two parts: first, an effort to establish and demonstrate cross-referencing ability (122 sessions in a period of 3½ months); second, an even more sustained effort to establish functional use of prepositions (intermittent training/testing over 2 years, including an intensive period of 126 training sessions in 3½ months).

Cross-Referencing Task

The cross-referencing task examines a child's ability to use established conditioned responses correctly in relation to a discriminative stimulus. The practical importance of this ability is apparent from everyday life. We are constantly confronted with an array of stimuli which have multiple dimensions, and to which multiple responses are possible. We rely on the various antecedent or contextual cues (discriminative stimuli) to make a

Table 6. Leon: Cross-Referencing (Auditory S^D), Sessions 101, 103, 110

Session	Trial	S^D	Response	Session	Trial	S^D	Response
101	24	C-R1	R	103	53	C-R1	R
	25	C-Y1	Y		54	O-Y□	Y
	26	O-R□	R		55	"	□
	27	"	□		56	O-R□	R
	28	O-R1	1		57	"	□
	29	O-R1	1		58	O-R□	□
	30	O-Y□	□		59	O-Y□	□
	31	O-R1	1		60	O-R1	1
	32	C-Y1	1		61	O-R1	1
	33	"	Y		62	O-Y1	1
	34	C-Y□	Y		63	C-R□	R□
	⋮				64	"	□
	51	O-R□	□		65	"	R
	52	O-R1	R		66	C-R1	1
	53	"	1		67	"	R
110	1	O-BO	O		68	C-Y□	□
	2	C-YO	Y		69	"	Y□
	⋮				70	"	□
	24	C-BO	B		71	"	□
	25	C-Y□	□		72	"	□
	26	"	□		73	"	□
	27	"	Y		74	"	Y
					75	C-Y□	Y

response which is likely to be positively reinforced. A response which is likely to be positively reinforced, i.e., "correct" or "appropriate," following one discriminative stimulus may not be reinforced or may be punished following a different discriminative stimulus. In common parlance, then, discriminative stimuli guide us in making "appropriate" responses on a given occasion. Autistic children often demonstrate types of responses which are precise, ordinary, and potentially useful in and of themselves, but which occur at times or under such circumstances that they appear to be meaningless or at least nonadaptive. Much of the behavior which supports both biological survival and social adaptation depends on the ability to selectively emit, from an enormous range of learned potential responses, a particular response under the control of a discriminative stimulus.

In the case of Leon, it had been clearly demonstrated that he could make consistent correct associations across all sensory modalities and for all parts of speech of the 9WL. In addition, he could accurately respond to 3-word "sentences." The question now was whether, in the presence of overlapping stimulus dimensions, Leon could select a particular dimension in response to a discriminative stimulus. Could he selectively name either shape only or color only on request?

The initial cross-referencing task for Leon was to name only the shape or only the color of a presented object when the discriminative stimulus was the spoken word "object" or "color."

We were surprised. After observing that Leon had practically no difficulty on any aspect of the 9WL, our expectation was that he would shortly master the cross-referencing task. He never did. The vicissitudes of our training/his

Table 7. Leon: Cross-Referencing (Auditory S^D), Session 105 (1:35–1:55 p.m.)

Trial	S^D	Response	Trial	S^D	Response	Trial	S^D	Response
1	C-R□	R	26	"	□	51	O-Y□	□
2	C-Y□	□	27	C-Y□	R	52	O-R□	□
3	"	Y	28	"	Y	53	C-Y1	Y
4	C-R1	R	29	C-Y1	Y	54	C-R□	R
5	C-Y1	Y	30	O-Y□	Y	55	O-Y1	1
6	C-R□	R	31	"	□	56	O-Y□	□
7	O-Y□	Y	32	O-Y□	Y	57	O-R1	R
8	"	□	33	"	□	58	"	1
9	O-R□	R	34	O-R1	R	59	O-Y□	Y
10	"	□	35	"	1	60	"	□
11	O-R1	R	36	O-Y1	Y	61	C-R1	R
12	"	1	37	"	1	62	C-Y1	Y
13	O-Y□	Y	38	O-R1	R	63	O-Y□	Y
14	"	□	39	"	1	64	"	□
15	O-R1	R	40	O-Y□	Y	65	O-R1	R
16	"	R	41	"	Y	66	"	1
17	"	1	42	"	□	67	O-Y□	Y
18	O-R□	□	43	O-R□	□	68	"	□
19	O-Y□	Y	44	O-R1	R	69	O-R1	R
20	"	□	45	"	1	70	"	1
21	O-R1	1	46	O-Y□	□	71	O-R□	R
22	O-Y1	Y	47	O-R□	R	72	"	□
23	"	1	48	"	□	73	C-Y□	Y
24	O-R□	R	49	O-Y1	Y	74	C-R1	R
25	"	R	50	"	1	75	C-Y1	1
						76	"	Y

learning over the next 122 sessions (3½ months) are illuminating. For once more, trial-by-trial examination of his responding disclosed shifting strategies and error patterns and motivational states. In addition, he again proved able to make much better use of visual discriminative stimuli than of auditory.

An early strategy was the simple one of "sticking with a winner." In this case, Leon would continue to respond to the object dimension or to the color dimension until such a response was not reinforced; then he would respond to the other dimension. Such a strategy might make sense in the face of certain nonrandom variations in the discriminative stimulus. (See Table 6, session 101, trials 24-34). At other times, he appeared to be using the object itself as a discriminative stimulus, rather than the word spoken by the adult. For example, if a red block were presented he would always respond to the shape dimension, whereas if a red stick were presented he would always respond to the color dimension. For a period, this was consistent regardless of the spoken discriminative stimulus. (See Table 6, session 101, trials 51-53.) At still other times, a rigidity of response was apparent. He would persist in responding to either the shape or color dimension despite repeated presentations of the other discrminative stimulus. In motivational terms, one might speculate about Leon's effort to control or force the outcome of his way. (See Table 6, session 103, trials 53-75.) This is also striking in session 105 (Table 7), where the set of responding to the color dimension seems strongly established but is combined with a minor strategy of responding to the shape dimension if the color dimension response is not reinforced. What is seen here is that he consisently responds to color unless the response is not reinforced. In this case, he switches on the next trial to a correct shape response and is reinforced. However, he now does not remain with the shape dimension but reverts to the color dimension on the following trial, i.e., he does not now "stick with a winner".

It is of interest that Leon's conditioned associations to the three colors and the three shapes were robust. That is, despite much nonreinforcement, he did not experiment with renaming colors or shapes as some children do under a condition of sustained failure (cf. *Jonathan*). If presented with a red block, he never said "blue" or "yellow" or "stick" or "ring." Colloquially, "What Leon is saying is true, but he is not answering the question!" (See Table 8, responses to "color" discriminative stimulus.)

Another perplexing observation is that when the discriminative stimulus was held constant at, say, "color" and Leon was consistently responding to the color dimension and being reinforced, he occasionally ("spontaneously") reverted to the shape dimension. That is, he kept "scanning the field," even though he was never getting "payoff" for shape responses. We might assume that eventually the shape response would extinguish—as, for example, it had when he so quickly learned the RV1 task. There appears to be some interplay

Table 8. Leon: Cross-Referencing (Auditory S^D), Session 104 (9:15–9:40 a.m.)

Trial	S^D	Response	Trial	S^D	Response	Trial	S^D	Response
1	C-R☐	R	26	"	1	51	C-R1	1
2	C-Y1	1	27	C-Y☐	Y	52	"	R
3	"	Y	28	C-R1	1	53	O-Y☐	Y
4	O-R1	R1	29	"	R	54	"	☐
5	"	R	30	O-R☐	R	55	O-R☐	R
6	"	R	31	"	☐	56	"	☐
7	"	1 (prompt)	32	C-Y1	1	57	C-Y1	Y
8	"	1	33	"	1	58	C-R1	1
9	O-Y☐	☐	34	"	Y	59	"	R
10	C-Y1	1	35	C-R1	R	60	O-Y☐	Y
11	"	Y	36	C-Y☐	☐	61	"	☐
12	O-R☐	R	37	"	Y	62	C-Y☐	☐
13	"	R	38	O-R1	R	63	"	Y
14	"	☐	39	"	R	64	O-R☐	☐
15	C-Y☐	☐	40	"	1	65	C-R☐	☐
16	"	Y	41	C-R☐	☐	66	"	R
17	O-Y1	Y	42	"	R	67	O-Y1	Y1
18	"	1	43	C-Y1	Y	68	"	1
19	O-R☐	R	44	O-Y☐	☐	69	C-R☐	R
20	"	☐	45	C-R1	1	70	O-R1	R
21	C-R1	1	46	"	1R	71	"	1
22	O-R1	R	47	"	1	72	C-Y☐	☐
23	"	R	48	"	R	73	"	Y
24	"	1	49	O-Y1	Y	74	O-Y1	1
25	O-Y1	Y1	50	"	1	75	C-Y☐	Y

here between an extinction schedule and the "scanning function." But perhaps the most parsimonious explanation of these phenomena is that Leon places primary reliance on visual cues rather than auditory ones. Most frequently, when he does make a correct shift in *set*, i.e., at the same time as the shift of the auditory discriminatory stimulus, his shift is found to occur when the stimulus object also has been changed. Conversely, when he switches *set* without a simultaneous switch in discriminative stimulus, that also is associated with a change in the stimulus object. (See Table 6, session 110 and Table 9.) In other words, visual information (the object presented) is prepotent over auditory information (the discriminative stimulus): Leon appears to "use" visual information and to "ignore" auditory information.[8]

Looking across all cross-referencing sessions, there appears to be an overall shift in the direction of simplifying response patterns. There is a certain economy here as if Leon might be saying, "If I can't win/succeed, I might as

[8]This raises a question of an error in training strategy—a not infrequent experience for us, in retrospect. By beginning the training with four objects (two colors and two shapes), there was more variety in visual stimuli than in the auditory stimuli. In addition, the color and shape dimension of the stimulus objects varied more or less independently of the varying auditory discriminative stimulus. Thus, there was no obvious labeling of the auditory discriminative stimulus as useful information. However, when we tried to rectify this by training, using just a single object, there was gradual improvement to only a 60% level of correct responding (sessions 115–134: 1,425 trials). And when all nine objects were reintroduced, the level of correct responding remained about the same.

Table 9. Leon: Cross-Referencing (Auditory S^D), Session 110 (9:15–9:45 a.m.)

Trial	S^D	Response	Trial	S^D	Response
26	C-Y□	□	51	C-Y⊙	⊙
27	"	Y	52	"	Y
28	C-B⊙	⊙	53	C-B□	□
29	"	B	54	"	B
30	C-Y□	□	55	C-B⊙	B
31	"	Y	56	C-Y□	□
32	C-B□	□	57	"	Y
33	"	□	58	C-Y⊙	Y
34	"	□	59	C-Y□	□
35	"	□	60	"	Y
36	"	B	61	C-B⊙	⊙
37	C-Y□	□	62	"	B
38	"	Y	63	C-B⊙	B
39	C-Y⊙	Y	64	C-B⊙	B
40	C-B⊙	B	65	C-B□	B
41	C-B□	B	66	C-B⊙	B
42	C-Y□	□	67	C-Y⊙	Y
43	"	Y	68	C-Y□	Y
44	C-B□	□	69	C-B□	B
45	"	B	70	C-B⊙	B
46	C-B□	B	71	C-Y□	□
47	C-Y□	□	72	"	□
48	"	Y	73	"	□
49	C-B⊙	⊙	74	"	Y
50	"	B	75	O-Y□	□

well get by as easily as possible." He did, at times, settle on response patterns which, while not maximizing his payoff, nevertheless did maintain a certain level of positive reinforcement (variable ratio 1.5/5). Introducing a 30 second time-out for incorrect responses did not improve his success/failure ratio. Rather, it resulted in behavioral signs of "ratio strain," such as increased latencies, inattention, silliness. This "negativism" was immediately eliminated by reprograming. For instance, reintroducing all 9 objects and reinforcing for color responses only promptly led to a session in which there were 75 consecutive correct responses.

There followed a training strategy in which red, yellow, and blue common objects other than the block, ring, and stick were used, e.g., plate, cup, truck, comb, etc. This was carried out for 24 sessions with no significant improvement: Success rate hovered around 60–70%.

The next training strategy was to use a visual discriminative stimulus. This was done by making an appropriate action with the object in question when an "object" response was wanted. For example, the adult would simulate drinking from a *cup*, throwing a *ball*, combing with a *comb*, etc. if an "object" response was wanted. If a color response was wanted, the object would simply be presented motionless. With such a visual discriminative stimulus, Leon immediately began performing with nearly 100% success! (See Table 10, session 169.) Gradually, variations on this visual discriminative stimulus were introduced. It was found that any action with an object, even inappropriate action such as "drinking from a comb," would still elicit a correct noun response, while no action continued to elicit a correct adjective response. An effort to control noun and adjective responses by an arbitrary visual discriminative stimulus for each (vertical motion of an object for color, horizontal motion of an object for noun) resulted in a decrease in correct responding to between 40 to 60% across 19 training sessions. Reintroduction of appropriate action for a noun promptly led to correct responses increasing to 90%. (See Table 10, session 219.)

Finally, it may be said that efforts to associate the usable visual discriminative stimuli (action with objects) with the auditory discriminative stimuli ("object" or "color") and then fading the visual discriminative stimulus were not successful. Through the end of training on the cross-referencing task (session 223), there was no evidence that Leon's noun or adjective responses were controlled by the auditory discriminative stimulus.

In summary, then, it appears that Leon possessed the ability to quickly learn the basic elements of the 9WL in all modalities and that he had difficulty in using a discriminative stimulus to select an "appropriate" response from among two "correct" alternatives. While he promptly did make good use of certain visual discriminative stimuli, we could never adduce evidence that he was making any use of auditory discriminative stimuli, i.e.,

Table 10. Leon: Cross-Referencing (Visual S^D), Sessions 169 and 219

	Session 169			Session 219	
Trial	S^D	Response	Trial	S^D	Response
26	O-B cup	cup	26	O-Y cup	cup
27	O-B cup	arms	27	O-R □	□
28	C-Y bead	Y	28	O-R cup	cup
29	O-Y bead	Y	29	C-Y leg	Y
30	"	Y	30	O-B car	car
31	"	bead	31	O-Y leg	leg
32	O-R cup	cup	32	C-R bead	R
33	C-B cup	B	33	O-B arm	arms
34	C-R truck	R	34	C-R cup	R
35	O-Y leg	leg	35	O-B car	car
36	C-B car	B	36	C-R bead	bead
37	C-Y bead	Y	37	"	R
38	O-R bead	bead	38	O-B cup	cup
39	C-B arm	B	39	C-Y cup	Y
40	C-Y cup	Y	40	O-Y bead	bead
41	O-B car	car	41	C-B cup	B
42	C-R truck	R	42	O-B arm	arms
43	O-Y cup	cup	43	C-R cup	R
44	C-R cup	R	44	O-R □	□
45	O-B arm	arm	45	C-Y leg	Y
46	C-R bead	R	46	O-R bead	bead
47	O-Y bead	bead	47	C-B car	B
48	C-B car	B	48	C-Y leg	Y
49	O-R bead	bead	49	O-B cup	cup
50	O-Y leg	leg	50	O-Y leg	leg

he was not integrating auditory and visual information. It is possible that with further auditory training employing more conspicuous auditory discriminative stimuli (for instance, buzzer and no buzzer) that Leon's responses might have come under control of an auditory stimulus. Regardless, it seems clear that Leon had significant impairment of his ability to use verbal auditory discriminative stimuli beyond what one would expect in a normal child, even though his auditory-visual and auditory-vocal associations were demonstrably faultless on the 9WL. Rather than pursuing this further, we turned to training Leon on another element of language, namely prepositions.

Prepositions and Syntax

Prepositions represent a linguistic element which ordinarily begins to be acquired shortly after the second birthday. Since they depict the relationships between things, prepositions are essential for rich communication and also require some ability to abstract if their relational referents are to be realized, i.e., if they are to have more than simple signal value. Despite the fact that Leon had not demonstrated ability to cross-reference, he had mastered all elements of the 9WL, and his adequacy on the generalization tests suggested some ability to abstract. Developmentally, his mental age, according to various measures, was well into the range where prepositions are normally acquired. For more than 2 years, occasional efforts had been made to teach Leon the proper use, both receptively and expressively, of a few prepositions: *in, on, under, beside.* It was found that under very limited circumstances he could make correct responses to prepositions and could use them to correctly "describe" relationships between things. However, the circumstances under which such performance could be demonstrated were so restricted as to suggest that these verbal elements never acquired more than signal value for Leon, and there was no evidence that prepositions had acquired semantic or syntactic value.

Approaches to training Leon in the use of prepositions varied widely. At times, the objects used and the setting were those of everyday life, and the approach used was flexible and limited only by the imagination of the adult. For example, an adult would play with Leon or take him on walks, and in the course of these pleasant activities look for opportunities to use prepositions, receptively and expressively, in spontaneous, naturally appropriate and useful ways. At other times, the objects were those of the 9WL, and the training format was highly formalized and employed the various operant conditioning procedures which had proven to be most effective with other types of training. At such times, stimulus, response, and consequence were recorded trial by trial.

On four occasions spanning 14 months, Leon was given a preposition test in an effort to analyze his performance, disclose his error patterns, and suggest guidelines for further training. The four tests were identical. The procedure was as follows:

> With breakfast withheld, Leon worked for bites of his lunch. On a small table were four objects: a plate, a cup, a fork, a shoe. After demonstrating consistently correct auditory-visual and visual-vocal responses to these objects, Leon was presented 101 randomized trials: The adult would say, "Put [object] in/on/under/beside [object]." Leon would repeat verbatim this auditory stimulus and then be allowed to follow the given instruction. If he arranged two objects in accord with the instruction, the adult would respond with verbal acknowledgement and a food reinforcer. If his response was incorrect, the adult would simply say, "No," and no food would be given. In either case, Leon was then asked, "Where is [direct object]?" If Leon

correctly described the existing relationship of the object just inquired about (even if he had responded incorrectly to the initial instruction), his "description" would again be acknowledged as correct, and another bit of food would be offered. If, as was often the case, he simply echoed the initial instruction so that it did not accurately describe the arrangement he had made, no reward was given. (In randomizing trials, instructions impossible to follow, e.g., "put plate in shoe," were excluded.) The tests were then examined in terms of Leon's "action errors" and "description errors."

The results are examined more closely below, but here it can be noted that although there were some striking shifts in the types of errors made, none of the changes in training strategy led to mastery of the 4-word sentence paradigm, "Put [object] in/on/under/beside [object]." For example, at the time of the first preposition test Leon was making few errors concerning prepositions per se; he made many errors in selecting either the direct object or the object of the preposition. When further training focused on correcting this defect, he was found, on later preposition tests, to have decreased the errors in selecting objects, but now he was making more errors on prepositions themselves. When training attention focused on one or two prepositions with which he was having special trouble, his performance here would improve, but he would begin making more errors on prepositions to which he had previously responded with consistent correctness (a phenomenon observed in, for example, *Carl* and *Stan* on other tasks).

Leon's errors on the four preposition tests can be examined under two broad categories, action errors and description errors. All of his action errors, in turn, can be accounted for in five categories:

(1) Preposition Errors (PE), e.g., responds to, "Put shoe beside cup" by putting shoe *in* cup.

(2) Reversal of Object Errors (R/O), e.g., responds to, "Put shoe on fork" by placing *fork* on *shoe*.

(3) Direct Object Errors (DO), e.g., responds to, "Put fork beside plate" by placing *cup* beside plate.

(4) Object of Preposition Errors (OP), e.g., responds to, "Put cup beside plate" by placing cup beside *shoe*.

(5) Beside Cup Rigidity (BC), e.g., responds to, "Put shoe beside plate" by putting shoe *beside cup*, or responds to, "put shoe in cup" by placing shoe *beside cup*. This is reminiscent of, the "monolithism" described above concerning Carl.

Description errors are considered in only two categories:

(1) Echo Errors (EE)—errors in which Leon echoes the original instruction (auditory stimulus) even though it does not accurately

Table 11. Leon: Comparison of Four Preposition Tests

Preposition	Trials	Errors of all types			
		PT1	PT2	PT3	PT4
		← 3 months →	← 8 months →	← 3 months →	
In	10	7	1	1	1
On	29	20	15	23	13
Under	35	30	34	36	35
Beside	27	15	11	25	16
Total	101	72	61	85	67

	By type of error			
	PT1	PT2	PT3	PT4
	Total	Total	Total	Total
Action errors	54 (15)	61 (2)	82 (9)	58 (0)
In	4 (1)†	1 (0)	0 (0)	2 (0)
On	15 (7)	15 (1)	23 (0)	10 (0)
Under	23 (3)	34 (1)	36 (6)	34 (0)
Beside	12 (4)	11 (0)	23 (3)	12 (0)
Description errors	57 (18)	59 (0)	76 (3)	67 (9)
In	6 (3)†	1 (0)	1 (1)	3 (1)
On	13 (5)	14 (0)	23 (0)	13 (3)
Under	27 (7)	33 (0)	30 (0)	35 (1)
Beside	11 (3)	11 (0)	22 (2)	16 (4)
Combined A&D errors	39	59	73	58
In	3	1	0	2
On	8	14	23	10
Under	20	33	30	34
Beside	8	11	20	12
Echo errors	19	47	67	48
In	0	0	0	2
On	1	7	19	8
Under	12	30	30	30
Beside	6	10	18	8
Prep errors	11	40	80	43
In	1	1	0	2
On	3	7	22	6
Under	7	32	36	34
Beside	0	0	22	1

+Same response (double scoring).

†Numbers in parentheses indicate action or description errors alone, without associated description or action errors, respectively.

Table 11. (cont'd)

		By type of error							
		PT1 Total		PT2 Total		PT3 Total		PT4 Total	
R/O errors		27		28		39		23	
In			0		0		0		0
On			8		7		11		5
Under			14		12		19		9
Beside			5		9		9		9
DO errors		14		4		1		9	
In			2		0		0		0
On			4		1		0		2
Under			5		1		0		4
Beside			3		2		1		3
OP errors		14		4		0		6	
In			3		0		0		0
On			5		1		0		2
Under			6		1		0		4
Beside			6+		2		0		3
BC rigidity		11		0		4		0	
In			1		0		0		0
On			2		0		2		0
Under			2		0		2		0
Beside			6+		0		0		0
Action errors/trial									
In	1		1		1		0		1
	2		3		0		0		1
	3		0		0		0		0
		4		1		0		2	
On	1		11		14		13		7
	2		3		0		10		2
	3		1		1		0		1
		15		15		23		10	
Under	1		15		23		17		21
	2		6		10		19		12
	3		2		1		0		1
		23		34		36		34	
Beside	1		10		9		14		8
	2		2		2		9		4
	3		0		0		0		0
		12		11		23		12	
All preps	1		37		47		44		37
	2		14		12		38		19
	3		3		2		0		2
		54		61		82		58	

describe the action he had just taken; e.g., in response to "Put shoe on plate," Leon may put the shoe beside the fork. When asked, "Where is shoe?" he responds, "Shoe on plate."

(2) All other description errors regardless of the correctness or incorrectness of his action response.

On any trial, Leon made from 0 to 3 action errors. His performance on all four preposition tests is summarized in the accompanying table.

Overall performance: Leon's best overall performance is on preposition test #1 (PT1), worst on PT3, and about the same on PT2 and PT4. His response to the preposition *in* shows overall improvement after PT1, and this is maintained on all subsequent tests, i.e., he appears to have learned and maintained correct responses to this particular preposition. It is also seen that maximum R/O errors are generally associated with maximum preposition errors. After mastering the preposition *in*, he makes no further R/O, DO, or BC errors associated with this preposition, and only one OP error. It is as if he really "knows" *in* and makes no associated errors. Where he has most trouble with a preposition, such as *under*, he makes many more R/O errors, and these errors persist even though other errors associated with *under* disappear or become very infrequent. BC rigidity errors also drop out after PT1 and rarely recur. Thus, it appears that preposition and R/O errors are the ones that persist in spite of intervening training, and they especially persist for certain prepositions. PT3 displays Leon's worst performance, and here there is a striking increase in the frequency of two-errors per trial. There is a twofold to fourfold increase compared with PT1, PT2, and PT4 for all prepositions except *in*. By the end of Leon's training and PT4, he has fairly well mastered three of the prepositions and is doing very poorly on the fourth (*under*). However, his R/O errors show little change. Other errors have practically disappeared.

Comparing PT2 with PT1 there is a 15% decrease in total errors (72 to 61) despite a marked increase in preposition errors (11 to 40). This overall decrease in errors is largely attributable to the elimination of BC errors and a marked reduction in DO and OP errors. R/O errors are virtually unchanged. The increase in preposition errors is almost entirely accounted for by incorrect responses to the preposition *under* (32 errors in 35 trials in PT2, compared to only 7 errors in the same 35 trials in PT1). Half of these 32 errors involve an *on* response to the instruction *under*. No such errors had been made in PT1. There is also a shift in the relationship between action and description errors when PT2 is compared to PT1. On 54 action errors in PT1, 15 occurred without accompanying description errors, i.e., Leon responded incorrectly to the auditory instruction but correctly "described" the action he had taken. Out of 57 description errors in the same test, 18 occurred without

Table 12. Leon: Preposition Errors (21 Sessions)

Trials	Total errors	Single errors			Double errors	
		PE only	DO only	OP only	P + OP	DO + P
1,229	535	495	2	15	19	4

accompanying action errors, i.e., Leon responded correctly to the auditory instruction and then inaccurately "described" the arrangement he had made. Thus, in PT1 almost a third of the action and description errors are dissociated from each other. In contrast, on PT2 (and PT3 and PT4) there is virtually no such dissociation: Virtually all action errors are associated with description errors and vice versa. This phenomenon is largely explained when we examine Leon's echo errors, for these increase two and a half times in PT2 and now constitute 80% of his description errors. In other words, he seems to have established a *set* of echoing the auditory instruction regardless of his action response.

Prior to PT3, exact stimuli and responses were recorded for 21 sessions. Leon was instructed to, "Put [common object] in/on/under/beside table/ chair/box/floor." There was no effort to randomize the direct objects, the prepositions, or the objects of the prepositions, but Leon had extensive training on all reasonable[9] combinations of the basic sentence. It was first established that he could consistently identify all objects included in the requests. That is, he was known to make accurate and consistent auditory-visual associations to each object. Working with two different adults, Leon ranged between one-third and two-thirds correct responses, averaging 56% overall. There was no evidence of sustained improvement despite shifts in training strategy. A summary of his performance is presented in Table 12.

Out of 535 total errors, 495 (or almost 93%) were errors in response to the stimulus preposition only, and these errors were quite evenly distributed across the 4 prepositions. On only two occasions did Leon respond correctly to the preposition and object of the preposition but incorrectly to the object of the verb. On another 15 trials he responded correctly to the object of the verb and preposition but incorrectly to the object of the preposition. On another 23 trials he made "double" errors, i.e., he responded incorrectly to both the preposition and either the object of the verb or the object of the

[9]For instance, he was never asked to "put table beside floor."

preposition (usually the latter). Thus, his errors in properly identifying the object at hand (and associating to the nouns of the sentence) were relatively rare overall; practically all of his errors reflected an inability to relate these objects accurately to each other in response to spoken prepositions.

Errors involving substantives were infrequent, and there were none of the reversal of object errors which were so conspicious on the first two preposition tests. This is probably because the direct objects were small movable objects and the objects of prepositions were large objects which were impossible or relatively difficult to move.

PT3, administered 8 months after PT2, marks Leon's worst measured performance throughout the 14-month period. Although BC, OP, and DO errors are now practically nonexistent, all other types of errors are markedly increased. Whereas he had infrequently or never made errors on the prepositions *on* and *beside* on previous preposition tests, he now misses almost all of these prepositions. There is an accompanying but smaller increase in R/O errors. These errors again reflect a kind of rigidity or "monolithism" which is reminiscent of the BC rigidity. For example, when the direct object is *plate* or *cup*, Leon's response almost always displays a reversal of the direct object and the object of the preposition (R/O error), whereas if the direct object in the instruction is *fork* or *shoe* such a reversal does not occur. It is as if forks and shoes can be "put" in relation to another object, but plates and cups cannot. As before, the frequency of R/O errors is greatest in association with prepositions with which Leon also makes the most errors. He correctly describes 9 of his 82 action errors and on only three occasions does he incorrectly describe a correct action. Thus, almost 90% of his errors include the wrong action and wrong description, and over 90% of these description errors are of the echo type, i.e., he is simply parroting the initial instruction rather than describing the arrangement he has made. The other striking thing about PT3 is the marked increase in the number of trials in which he is making two different types of action error per trial: 38, as compared to 14 in PT1 and 12 in PT2.

Because of Leon's apparent lack of progress, dramatically clear after PT3, a decision was made to simplify and formalize the training still further in order to better understand his error patterns and to more closely guide our training efforts.

Leon had 80 training sessions over the next 2 months in which the objects of the 9WL were used. The same 4-word sentence paradigm and operant conditioning methods were employed, but the stimulus array was limited to two objects at a time, designated by either color or shape, and a single preposition (*beside*). We gradually worked toward using all nine objects of the 9WL—designating these objects by both color and shape—and toward using two prepositions (*beside, on*). In the final phase, we again introduced small common objects.

Using this procedure, Leon mastered, "put [color] beside [color]," then "put [shape] beside [shape]," and finally "put [color + shape] beside [color + shape]" within six training sessions. By this time, all nine 9WL objects were included in the stimulus array. By now, however, because of the use of only one preposition (*beside*), Leon's "beside" response was set, so that the task really amounted to a conjunction involving the auditory-visual mode. That is, an instruction such as, "Put yellow ring beside blue stick" really involved a challenge no different than "Put yellow ring and blue stick in box." In other words, the attention to the relationship of the two objects demanded by the preposition had effectively been absorbed into a stereotyped motor response. The interesting question was what would happen when the *relationship* demand was reimposed by the addition of a second preposition. We had an opportunity to observe these effects at three different points in the subsequent training:

(1) Session 33—having established consistently correct responses to a single preposition (*beside*), we now repeated the training procedure always using the preposition *on*.

(2) Session 48 and 49—once Leon was consistently correct in responding to the preposition *on*, these two prepositions, *on* and *beside*, were admixed.

(3) Session 66—following a 14-day holiday break, Leon was switched from an *on* only task to a *beside* only task.

Session 33: When the preposition *on* was introduced after overtraining with the preposition *beside*, Leon first experimented by reversing the direct object and object of the preposition. However, within two trials he switched to an "on" response and rarely missed the preposition thereafter. As the relevant stimulus domain contained only two objects and one preposition, the only types of errors possible were either preposition errors or R/O errors. However, over the next 12 sessions, Leon never achieved more than an 81% success rate. Most of his errors were of the R/O type, and sometimes he would persist in stereotyped incorrect R/O errors for several trials in a row. Preposition errors ("beside" rather than "on") occurred only in the process of "experimenting" after an R/O type error, i.e., Leon varied the preposition rather than the direct object and object of the preposition. Finally, when a third block was introduced, thus providing three rather than two stimulus colors, Leon suddenly made only one error on two consecutive sessions! (This is one of several occasions on which an apparent increase in complexity of stimulus array actually resulted in improved performance.)

Sessions 48 and 49: For the first time in this training sequence, the prepositions *on* and *beside* were used together in the same session. The stimulus array consisted of a red, a yellow, and a blue block. Leon was thus

Table 13. Leon: Prepositions, Session 48

Trial	S^D	Response	Trial	S^D	Response	Trial	S^D	Response
1	B/R	B/R	26	B/Y	B/Y	51	B/Y	BbY
2	Y/B	Y/B	27	BbR	B/R	52	"	B/Y
3	R/B	R/B	28	"	R/B	53	RbB	R/B
4	B/Y	B/Y	29	"	BbR	54	"	RbB
5	R/Y	R/Y	30	RbY	R/Y	55	R/Y	R/Y
6	B/R	B/R	31	"	Y/R	56	BbY	B/Y
7	B/Y	B/Y	32	"	RbY	57	"	BbY
8	R/Y	R/Y	33	BbR	BbR	58	RbY	RbY
9	B/R	B/R	34	Y/R	YbR	59	Y/R	YbR
10	Y/B	Y/B	35	"	Y/R	60	"	Y/R
11	R/B	R/B	36	B/Y	B/Y	61	BbR	BbR
12	R/Y	R/Y	37	RbY	RbY	62	R/Y	R/Y
13	Y/B	Y/B	38	Y/R	Y/R	63	RbY	YbR
14	B/Y	B/Y	39	BbR	BbR	64	"	RbY
15	Y/B	Y/B	40	Y/B	Y/B	65	BbY	B/Y
16	R/B	R/B	41	R/Y	RbY	66	"	BbY
17	B/Y	B/Y	42	"	R/Y	67	B/Y	B/Y
18	R/Y	R/Y	43	B/R	B/R	68	BbY	BbY
19	R/B	R/B	44	Y/B	Y/B	69	R/Y	RbY
20	Y/B	Y/B	45	R/Y	R/Y	70	"	R/Y
21	B/R	B/R	46	YbR	Y/B	71	BbR	BbR
22	R/Y	R/Y	47	"	B/Y	72	Y/B	YbB
23	YbR	Y/R	48	"	R/Y	73	"	Y/B
24	"	R/Y	49	"	YbR	74	RbY	R/Y
25	"	YbR	50	BbR	BbR	75	"	RbY

Capital letters = colors; / = "on"; b = "beside."

instructed to "put [color] on/beside [color]." In effect, the introduction of two prepositions in a single training session now forced Leon to pay attention not only to the two substantives (direct object and object of the preposition) but also to make an auditory discrimination between the two prepositions so as to correctly relate two of three objects. His initial errors consisted of three identical sets of three trials each. (See Table 13, session 48, trials 23–32.) His response sequence was this: On the first trial he "ignored" the preposition, i.e., he responded as though to the previous correct prepositional response. On the second trial he again "ignored" the preposition (still staying with the last reinforced prepositional response) and made an R/O error, i.e., he reversed the direct object and object of the preposition. Thus, on the second trial he made

Table 14. Leon: Prepositions, Session 49

Trial	S^D	Response	Trial	S^D	Response	Trial	S^D	Response
1	RbY	R/Y	26	BbY	BbY	51	"	R/B
2	"	RbY	27	B/Y	B/Y	52	BbY	BbY
3	Y/B	Y/B	28	RbB	R/B	53	Y/B	Y/B
4	BbY	B/Y	29	"	RbB	54	BbY	BbY
5	"	BbY	30	RbB	RbB	55	R/Y	R/Y
6	RbY	RbY	31	B/R	RbB	56	BbR	B/R
7	Y/R	YbR	32	"	B/R	57	"	RbB
8	"	Y/R	33	YbB	Y/B	58	"	B/R
9	YbB	Y/B	34	"	YbB	59	"	RbB
10	"	YbB	35	B/Y	Y/B	60	"	BbR
11	R/Y	R/Y	36	"	BbY	61	B/R	BbR
12	BbR	BbR	37	"	BbY	62	"	B/R
13	Y/B	YbB	38	"	BbY	63	YbR	Y/R
14	"	Y/B	39	"	B/Y	64	"	YbR
15	YbB	YbB	40	BbY	B/Y	65	B/Y	B/Y
16	R/Y	R/Y	41	"	BbY	66	RbB	R/B
17	YbR	Y/R	42	R/B	R/B	67	"	RbB
18	"	YbR	43	BbY	B/Y	68	Y/R	Y/R
19	B/R	BbR	44	"	B/Y	69	BbR	RbB
20	"	B/R	45	"	BbY	70	"	R/B
21	YbR	YbR	46	Y/B	YbB	71	"	BbR
22	B/R	BbR	47	"	Y/B	72	Y/B	BbY
23	"	B/R	48	BbY	B/Y	73	"	B/Y
24	R/B	R/B	49	"	BbY	74	"	BbY
25	YbR	Y/R	50	R/B	RbY	75	"	YbB
						76	"	Y/B

Capital letters = colors; / = "on"; b = "beside."

two separate errors. On the third trial, Leon responded correctly. Thereafter, Leon made few errors in session 48 and usually to the preposition only, which error was immediately corrected on the subsequent trial. In session 49, Leon did not confuse DO and OP in the first 30 trials. He did, however, make 9 errors on prepositions which he immediately corrected in the next trial. Thereafter, when he made an error he began either to change his prepositional response or to reverse the DO and OP. Usually he experimented with only one change at a time, i.e., he would switch a prepositional response, and if that was not correct he would reverse DO and OP. In trials 70–74 he made three double switches after an incorrect response. It is apparent that within this rather simple paradigm, Leon's strategy for correcting errors was quite systematic and "intelligent," not random. His response to substantives did not decay. Nevertheless, he did not seem to be "learning" from his errors or even from his own corrective strategy.

Session 66: Training proceeded with a focus on helping Leon make simultaneous discriminations between two prepositions as well as between DO and OP. Session 66 represents another point at which the task was changed from one demanding only *on* responses to one demanding only *beside* responses. The striking thing is that almost without exception Leon now took four trials to make a correct response, i.e., he first made a preposition error, than a R/O error, then a preposition plus a R/O error together, and finally emitted the correct response. In other words, he was now making every possible mistake before responding correctly—and, again, making mistakes very systematically! At this point, Leon was acting as if he could consider only one change at a time, either a change in prepositional response or a reversal of DO and OP, but not both.

In *Session 67, beside* was still the only preposition used. By this time, Leon was making only preposition errors. That is, he was no longer reversing DO and OP. Yet, he recurrently made *on* prepositional responses, never staying with a correct *beside* response more than two trials in a row. The *beside* set was not established until Session 73! Once this was accomplished, Leon did very well using all nine objects of the 9WL in conjunction with the single preposition *beside.*

Next, with one block fixed to the table, Leon was asked to place a second block *on* or *beside* it. He quickly responded with 100% correctness! He made only one error in three sessions.

Sessions 86-103: By means of minutely programmed steps of successive approximation, Leon was able to reach criterion (22 correct responses out of a block of 25 trials in 2 consecutive sessions) using the paradigm, "put [adjective + noun] *on/beside* [adjective + noun]" and including all 9 objects of the 9WL. It thus appeared that Leon might at last have mastered the task of making differential responses to simultaneously changing substantives and prepositions.

Sessions 104-111: We now changed from the 9WL objects to common objects (three at a time) and two prepositions (still *on* and *beside*). Each of these last sessions was begun with 10 trials using the 9WL material which Leon had just mastered in sessions 86-103. Leon never met criterion as previously defined, although on different occasions his success/trial ratio was 15/15, 24/25, and 20/25. His errors on this last training sequence are represented in Table 15.

Because of other clinical considerations, Leon's formal training in prepositions was ended here with the administration of PT4. His performance on this final preposition test, while much better than his performance on PT3,

Table 15. Leon: Preposition Errors, Sessions 104–111

	Trials	Total errors	R/O	Prep	DO	OP
Number	389	102	76	16	2	3
Percent	–	26	74	16	2	3

R/O = reversal of objects; DO = direct object; OP = object of preposition.

was almost indistinguishable from his performance on PT2 11 months earlier. Almost a year of quite intensive training had led to no demonstrable progress. He continued to make mostly preposition errors (especially in response to *under*, concerning which there had been little training), together with persistent R/O errors. In addition, there were a few more DO and OP errors than there had been on either of the previous two preposition tests. (See Table 11.)

In summary, we tried. And Leon tried. Tasks which he could do at all he did quickly, willingly, almost flawlessly. So it was throughout the 9WL and, under extraordinarily defined conditions, even for tiny parts of the cross-referencing and preposition tasks. But concerning the latter tasks we must conclude that Leon was stretched beyond his abilities. His difficulty in integrating auditory and visual information seems inescapable from the cross-referencing work. Despite all efforts with prepositions during 2 years of work, we basically were unable to do more than simply rearrange errors. Leon's errors were usually patterned, not random. Perhaps the most significant finding out of that work is that Leon could make differential responses to a varying preposition, AND he could make differential responses to a varying substantive; however, he seemed unable to cope with simultaneous changes in BOTH. Some people, it is said, "can't walk and chew gum at the same time." We will soon see that another fully verbal autistic child, *Jonathan*, although spared Leon's difficulty with cross-referencing tasks and prepositions, eventually falls short of functional language—and flounders in essentially the same way as Leon.

JONATHAN

Jonathan was 7 years 9 months of age at the midpoint of training with the 9WL. He was an attractive blond boy with an unremarkable gestational and perinatal history. Although motor developmental milestones were passed at

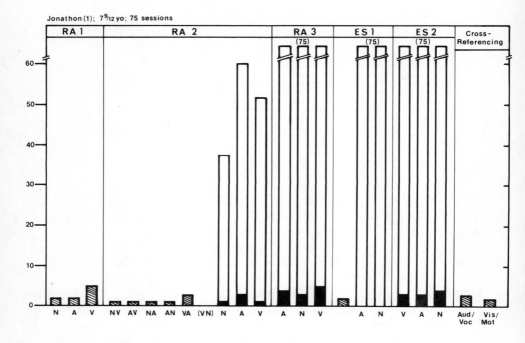

FIG. 17. Jonathan's histogram (1). (For legend, see Figs. 2 and 5.)

the appropriate times, Jonathan failed to develop speech beyond a few words and phrases, and these seemed to have no meaning for him. He was diagnosed as an autistic child. IQ, as estimated from the Draw-A-Person Test, was 57. On the Peabody Picture Vocabulary Test his IQ was 33, and a Stanford-Binet Test disclosed an IQ of 32. His social rating was 5, i.e., he avoided interaction most of the time. The history and initial examination, as well as our experience in treating Jonathan over a 2-year period, consistently gave evidence of his motor performance being considerably higher than his verbal competence. He could perform rather stereotyped but precise motor acts quite well (drawing houses, building with Lincoln logs). Although he could learn many things in a rote way, little of his learned behavior seemed to add anything to his mastery of the world. He continued to be stimulus-bound, unable to carry out complex behavior in order to reach a distant goal. His speech was generally clear and distinct but almost always echolalic. Several EEGs were always markedly abnormal.

On the 9WL, Jonathan had very little difficulty, especially on the receptive

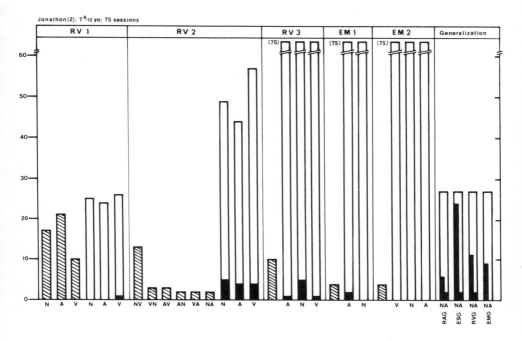

Jonathon (2); 7 ^{9}/12 yo; 75 sessions

FIG. 18. Jonathan's histogram (2). (For legend, see Figs. 2 and 5.)

auditory and expressive speech portions. He met criteria on all tasks with a minimum of training and made practically no mistakes on the post-tests.

Upon being presented with the receptive visual tasks, Jonathan required more training. This is probably because he had had no previous exposure to such tasks, whereas his entire life could be considered a kind of training for the receptive auditory tasks. At any rate, Jonathan did show a good ability to learn this new task and made only 1 error in 75 trials on his post-test. (See Figure 18.) Initially on the RV2 task, noun-plus-verb (NV) task, there was a strong sequence effect; moreover, as Jonathan began responding correctly to the first element, his errors on the second element increased. But once the NV task was mastered, on each of the remaining five combinations of 2-word signs, Jonathan reached criterion almost immediately. Again, his post-test showed few errors. On RV3, he reached criterion after 10 blocks of 25 trials, and his post-test showed 7 errors in 75 randomized trials. For both EM1 and the EM2 tasks, Jonathan reached criterion in four training blocks and made two errors and no errors on the respective post-tests.

Thus, despite some interesting and familiar error-patterns, Jonathan demonstrated his ability to quickly learn and consistently perform the 9WL tasks—tasks which depend on simple auditory-visual, visual-vocal, visual-visual, and visual-motor associations. With most of these tasks, he seemed to require little more than to become familiar with what was to be expected of him, and he would then respond quickly, consistently, accurately.

On the generalization tests, which presumably require some ability to abstract, Jonathan made more errors. On each of the four generalization tests, he made more errors than he had on any of his previous post-tests. (See Figure 18.) Interestingly, he never made more than 2 errors with adjectives, and on one generalization test (EMG) he made no adjective errors in 27 trials. He did, however, make between 9 and 24 noun errors out of 27 noun trials on each of the 4 generalization tests. These errors are somewhat difficult to interpret. On the RAG, for instance, after making no errors in 14 trials, he began responding to most noun stimuli by selecting a red, yellow, or blue object from the stimulus array even though the shape of these objects bore no resemblance to the object asked for (stick, block, or ring). Shortly thereafter, on the ESG generalization test, there was an even clearer indication that Jonathan's many errors were related to breaking his 9WL "set." For on this test, requiring a vocal response, rather than responding "block," "stick," or "ring," Jonathan once named the object itself (box) and thereafter regularly gave the color of the object even though it was not one of the 9WL colors. This occurred despite the fact that each generalization test is begun with six trials using the 9WL objects in an effort to establish the proper response set, and despite the fact that Jonathan did, in fact, correctly respond "ring" to the first novel object presented to him.

The fact remains, however, that Jonathan was clearly "taking" some test other than that which we were "administering," so it cannot be inferred with confidence that these tests demonstrate inability to generalize. However, such an inference would be consistent with all other observations about Jonathan's behavior. This is especially interesting when considered in relation to our efforts (described below) to move beyond echolalic speech. On RVG and EMG, administered about a month later, Jonathan was no longer giving color responses to a noun stimulus. Almost all of his errors continued to be nouns, but they now appeared to be simply incorrect choices, rather than "good" choices using the wrong set of rules. Since 60 of his 66 errors on all 4 generalization tests (91%) occurred on nouns rather than on adjectives, one might infer that it was more difficult for Jonathan to generalize from the shape than the color of the training objects. This conclusion has some common sense appeal, since the colors of the red, yellow, or blue novel objects used on the generalization tests were rather close in hue to the colors of the training objects. Thus, by selectively ignoring the shapes of such novel objects, there was really little "generalization" from the original objects required. In contrast, the shape of the novel objects could be thought of as more dissimilar from the shapes of the training objects, and many of them were undoubtedly familiar to Jonathan from past experience, e.g., a match box, a phonograph record, a pencil, etc.

Jonathan also had some training on cross-referencing tasks. In contrast to *Leon*, Jonathan quickly demonstrated proficiency at expressive vocal cross-referencing. When one of the 9WL objects was displayed, Jonathan would name the "color" or the "shape" as asked. Jonathan made 4 errors in the first 14 trials and then proceeded through 136 additional trials without error. We turned finally to an expressive motor cross-referencing task (EMC) in which a visual discriminative stimulus was presented (a card containing the letter C or the letter S) and a hand sign response from Jonathan was required. For this task, he required prompts on just the first three trials and then made no further errors. Thus, he had reached criterion on both of these cross-referencing tasks in minimum time. (See Figure 17.)

******

The remainder of Jonathan's language training which is considered here deals with an effort to help him progress from echolalic to spontaneous communicative speech. Other approaches to this were used in his treatment program, with some slight success. For instance, through a number of conditioning procedures, Jonathan did come to signal some of his wants in single words or short phrases. However, attention here is focused on our effort to directly teach some elements of "conversation" through drill with pronouns and simple statements and questions.

Syntax: Pronouns

Remember that by this time Jonathan displayed good speech: Voice quality, inflection, articulation, and vocabulary were all good. His rote memory was excellent. For instance, even before coming to the hospital he had memorized most of "The Night Before Christmas." At times, usually in response to visual stimuli, he would spontaneously "ask" for things in single words or short phrases. But most of his speech appeared to be either immediate or delayed echolalia. In other words, what he lacked was language—language as a tool for grasping reality and communicating. There was little indication that words had any meaning for Jonathan except as concrete labels. In other words, while he could make simple associations between words and visualized things, his spontaneous utterances gave no evidence of ability to generate novel sentences.

In trying to convert Jonathan's echolalic speech to functional language, we used methods similar to those described by Risley and Wolf (1967). We worked not so much to expand Jonathan's vocabulary, but rather we tried to train him with various elements of syntax, such as questions, pronouns, prepositions, and comparatives.[10]   In synopsis, Jonathan learned a large number of verbal responses quite precisely. While it was possible to move beyond mere echolalia, even Jonathan's "functional speech" appeared to be no more than a set of programmed responses to certain stimulus questions or situations. This was most dramatically apparent in his answers to questions. At various times Jonathan was taught to answer questions about weather, about his clothes, about his "identity" and body parts, etc. Later, should Jonathan be asked questions about his clothes, he might respond with "weather" answers. It was as if he were giving the "right" set of answers but to the "wrong" set of questions. We had not moved the target in front of Jonathan's arrow.

Jonathan also demonstrated pronominal reversal. While we were able to break up the pattern of pure echolalia in this regard, we were unable to establish consistent appropriate use of pronouns. Our experience was consistent with the findings of Bartak and Rutter (1974).

Many of Jonathan's speech abilities and language limitations can be illustrated with the following tape transcript. In this brief demonstration session, I used a question-and-answer format beginning with questions which Jonathan had already been trained to answer, and then gradually introduced a few questions with which he probably had had no previous experience, although the people and things about which he was being asked were known to be familiar to him. Finally, I introduced some questions which require mastery of personal pronouns and auxiliary verbs.

Transcription of Taped Interview with Jonathan[11]

1. C: Good morning Jonathan
2. J: Morning Doctor Churchill

[10]We also did a certain amount of drilling on rote responses which contained potentially useful information, such as his name, address, and phone number. As one of the behavioral problems with Jonathan was his running away from home ("running nowhere," according to parents, and without any sense of street danger), we thought there might be potential usefulness in Jonathan's being able to give his name, address, and phone number by rote in response to appropriate questions. We also trained Jonathan to wait at the curb, to look both ways, and to tell us whether cars were coming.

[11] • each dot represents one second of silence
* represents poorly articulated or unintelligible vocalizations
# represents elided words
[ ] indicates editorial comments
§ Spontaneous, accurate descriptions of *visual* stimuli

3. C: How are you?
4. J: Fine.
5. C: What is your name?
6. J: My name is . Jonathan Barrington.
7. C: Where do you live, Jonathan?
8. J: 4916 North Larkin Street.
9. C: What is your phone number?
10. J: 8-2-9-7-0-3-4. .
11. C: What is your mother's name?
12. J: My mother's name is* Isabel.
13. C: Do you have any sisters? . . . . . Do you have any sisters?
14. J: (Mumbles) Do you have any sisters . . . .
15. C: Jonathan, do you have any brothers?.
16. J: Sisters?
17. C: Do you have any brothers?
18. J: Tom and Earl.
19. C: How old is Earl?. . .
20. J: Brother! . . .
21. C: How old is Earl? . . .
22. J: Thompson? . . . [discharged one year previously]
23. C: Earl Thompson?
24. J: Earl Thompson
25. C: Yes. How old is Earl Barrington? . .
26. J: Earl Thompson . . . .
27. C: What is Earl's mother's name?
28. J: His* mother's name . . . . is . . . . . mother's name is . . Jonath
       . . . . .
29. C: Jonathan . . what is your name?
30. J: My name is Jonathan Barrington.
31. C: What is your mother's name?
32. J: My mother's name is Isabel.
33. C: What is your brother's name?
34. J: Brother's name is Tom and Earl . .
35. C: What is Tom's mother's name? . .
36. J: Tom and Earl . . .
37. C: Where does Tom live? . . .
38. J: 4916 North Larkin Street
39. C: Where does Earl live? . .
40. J: 4916 North Larkin Street . . . .
41. C: What is Isabel's phone number?
42. J: 8297034 . . . .
43. C: How old are you?
44. J: Fine . .
45. C: How *old* are you? . . .
46. J: Fine* . . Jonathan Barrington . .
47. C: Jonathan, how old are you? . .

48. J: Jonathan Barrington[*] . . m[*]y name is Jonathan Barrington . . . .
49. C: Are you 10 years old?
50. J: A[*]re[*] you 10 years old? . . . . Yes I'm ten years old . . [actually eight years old]
51. C: What is *my* name?
52. J: My name is Jonathan Barrington
53. C: What is *my* name?
54. J: My name is Dr. Churchill
55. C: Right! Yes. Jonathan, what color is your shirt? [Jonathan's shirt has wide blue and white stripes of equal width]
56. J: My shirt .[#]. blue
57. C: Blue . . . . .
58. J: White?
59. C: Blue and white, yes. What color is my shirt? . . [Yellow with blue pinstripe]
60. J: Blue . . and white . .
61. C: What color is *my* shirt?
62. J: Your shirt . . [*]your shirt is blue . . . .
63. C: Touch my shirt . . . . No that's Jonathan's shirt, that's *your* shirt. Touch *my* shirt . . . . .
64. J: Touch my sh . . . .
65. C: Jonathan, touch *my* shirt . . . . . Touch *Don's* shirt . . Touch Don's shirt . . No, that's Jonathan's shirt. Touch *Don's* shirt . . Yes! That's Don's shirt. What color is Don's shirt?
66. J: .[*]Yellow
67. C: Yellow . . . and what? . .
68. J: [*]Blue
69. C: Yellow and blue, yes . . What color is *my* shirt? . .
70. J: Blue and white
71. C: No. *Your* shirt is blue and white
72. J: *Shirt is blue and white
73. C: Yes. What color is *my* shirt
74. J: Your shirt . . blue . .
75. C: Jonathan . . what color is *my* shirt? . . .
76. J: Yellow and blue
77. C: Your shirt
78. J: Is yellow and blue
79. C: Yes . . . Jonathan, what color is my shirt?
80. J: Your shirt . is . . yellow and blue
81. C: Yes. [20 sec.] What are you doing?
82. J: I[#]sitting in a chair
83. C: Yes. What am I doing? . . .
84. J: Dr. Churchill you[#]sitting in a chair
85. C: Yes . . . .
86. J: *Big* block. §
87. C: Yes

88. J: *Little* cup §
89. C: Yes. Jonathan . . . Jonathan sit down . . Jonathan, you are sitting down
90. J: Jonathan you are* sitting down
91. C: Jonathan you have a yellow block
92. J: This* is* is* a yellow block . .
93. C: I am standing up
94. J: ****standing up
95. C: I have a blue cup
96. J: I have a blue cup
97. C: Mmhm. Jonathan, what are you doing? . .
98. J: I . have a blue cup
99. C: No. Jonathan, what are *you* doing? . .
100. J: You . . . .*
101. C: Jonathan, what are you doing?
102. J: I have a
103. C: No, I am . . .
104. J: I
105. C: am.
106. J: blue
107. C: No I am
108. J: a yellow block
109. C: I am sitting down
110. J: I am* sitting down
111. C: Jonathan, what are you doing? . . .
112. J: I . . . I*#sitting down.
113. C: I am sitting down.
114. J: I'm sitting down.
115. C: Yes . . . . Jonathan what are you doing?
116. J: (I'm?)* pouring the apple juice. §
117. C: That's what *I* am doing. Jonathan, what are *you* doing? . .
118. J: Ah . . Dr. Churchill, you have a blue cup
119. C: No. Jonathan, what are *you* doing?
120. J: I am sitting in I am sitting in a chair
121. C: Yes, you are sitting in a chair . . . . Jonathan, what am I doing? [standing up] . . .
            (you?)*
122. J: Dr. Churchill (has?) a blue block [No blue *block* in room!]
123. C: No. Jonathan, what am I *doing*? . .
124. J: I . I am sitting in a chair
125. C: No . . Jonathan, What am *I* doing?
            (blue?)*
126. J: Dr. Churchill, you have (a?) block
127. C: No. you are standing up
128. J: Up.
129. C: Jonathan, what am I doing? . . . .

130. J: I . . Dr. Churchill, you are standing up
131. C: Yes . . . . Jonathan, what are you doing? . . .
132. J: Dr. Churchill is standing up . .
133. C: Dr. Churchill is standing up?
134. J: Dr. Churchill is standing up
135. C: UmHm. Jonathan, what are *you* doing?
136. J: Dr. Churchill*
137. C: No. Jonathan what are *you* doing?
138. J: I'm standing up
139. C: No. You are not standing up . . Jonathan, what are *you* doing? . .
140. J: I am sitting in a chair.
141. C: Yes. You are sitting in a chair . . . . Jonathan, what are you doing? . . . .
142. J: (What am I doing?) I am sitting in a chair
143. C: Yes. You are sitting in a chair . . . . What are *you* doing?
144. J: Dr. Churchill, I am sitting in a chair
145. C: Yes . . . . What am *I* doing?
146. J: Dr. Churchill you are standing . Dr. Churchill you are standing up
147. C: Yes. I am standing up. You are sitting in a chair, and I am standing up (Jonathan simultaneously echoes last sentence) . . . Jonathan, what am *I* doing?
148. J: I am sitting in the chair
149. C: Yes . . . . Jonathan, what do I have? [blue cup] . .
150. J: I have a block
151. C: No. Jonathan, what do *I* have?
152. J: Dr. Churchill, you are standing up
153. C: What do I *have*?
154. J: Dr. Churchill, you have a blue *block*?
155. C: A blue.
156. J: A blue *block*!
157. C: No what *is* this?
158. J: Blue *cup*!
159. C: Yes. Jonathan, what do I have?
160. J: A blue cup.
161. C: Yes [26 sec.] Jonathan, what do I have? . . . . . .
162. J: A . . blue cup
163. C: Yes . . . . Jonathan, what do you have? [yellow block] . . .
164. J: a blue cup . .
165. C: Jonathan, what do *you* have? . .
166. J: Dr. Churchill#a blue cup
167. C: No. Jonathan, what do *you* have?
168. J: I am standing up

169. C: No, you are not standing up . . . You are sitting in a *chair*.
170. J: You are sitting in a *chair* . .
171. C: Jonathan, what do you have? . . . . . Jonathan what do you have
172. J: I *am sitting in a chair
173. C: No what do you *have*?
174. J: You* have a block. I* . .
175. C: I.
176. J: have a block.
177. C: Have a yellow block, yes . . . . Jonathan, what do you have? . .
178. J: ***(I have a forehead?) . . .
179. C: Jonathan, what do you have?
180. J: I have a forehead . .
181. C: You have a . . . .
182. J: ***(Unintelligible).
183. C: Jonathan, what do *you* have? . .
184. J: I . I . st . . I . . I have a yellow block
185. C: Very good . . . . Jonathan, what are . . . Jonathan, what are you *doing*? . . . .
186. J: I have a yellow block . .
187. C: Jonathan, what are you *doing*? . . .
188. J: Dr. Churchill you are standing up
189. C: No Jonathan what are *you* doing?
190. J: Dr. Churchill you have a bl . block . . Ch* . you have a blue *cup*
191. C: Yes, I have a blue cup
192. J: I have a blue cup
193. C: Jonathan, what are you *doing*?
194. J: Dr. Churchill
195. C: No, I am . .
196. J: *(unintelligible) . . . .
197. C: Jonathan, what are *you* doing?
198. J: Dr. Churchill you have* a blue cup
199. C: Uhhuh. Let's listen to this . . .

Analysis of Transcript

At the beginning of this transcript, Jonathan speaks with good volume, a well-modulated voice, clear articulation, and a generally happy, singsong intonation. His first several responses (through item 12) are to questions which he has been asked many times and has been trained to answer. His responses are prompt, and his voice reflects no hesitation. As I begin introducing unfamiliar questions to Jonathan, his responses show longer latencies, hesitation or stumbling over choice of words, and the appearance of poor articulation or even unintelligible mumblings. Such decay is most evident at those points in the transcript where Jonathan appears to be having the greatest difficulty in making correct responses *and* is being pressured considerably by me to respond correctly.

In item 13, I first introduce an unfamiliar question, "Do you have any sisters?" Getting no answer, I repeat the question. (Jonathan probably does not know what a *sister* is.) His response is echolalia! He repeats the question. This appears to be one of two characteristic strategies used by Jonathan when faced with an unfamiliar question. He reverts either (a) to echolalia or (b) to a familiar "right" answer. I go on to ask if Jonathan has any brothers. Jonathan has already been trained to give his brothers' names, which he does here. However, he has probably not been asked before, "How old is Earl?" (item 19), and he never does answer this question. Instead, he gives the full name of another child who shares Jonathan's brother's first name—a child who had been discharged from the hospital more than a year previously!

Continuing (item 27), while Jonathan can give his own mother's name without hesitation, he stumbles in giving his brother's mother's name and finally "reverts to the familiar," i.e., he begins to give his own name.

With item 29, I again bring Jonathan back to familiar territory. I ask for his own name and the names of members of his family. His answers are again quick, and his voice is again sure. When asking for information about them which Jonathan already has concerning himself, his answers remain prompt and certain. However, it is not clear whether he is answering through "understanding" or whether he is responding to trigger words in the questions, e.g., "live?" and "phone number?".

When asked for his age in item 43, Jonathan responds as if I had asked, "How are you?" When the question is repeated, "How *old* are you?" (item 45), he again says, "Fine," hesitates, and then gives his own name (reverts to the familiar). Repeating the question gains only repetitions of his own name (the familiar)—and, finally, echolalia.

Asking Jonathan to tell me my name (item 51), introduces his difficulty with possessive pronouns. This difficulty continues as I try to get him to name the colors in his own shirt and in my shirt. Despite the fact that Jonathan can name colors very well, he shows great difficulty in using the possessive pronouns (*your* shirt vs. *my* shirt) as discriminative stimuli. (This type of difficulty is reminiscent of the cross-referencing difficulty displayed by *Leon*.) There is every reason to believe that Jonathan's difficulty does not lie with confusion about colors, but rather with what colors, i.e., whose shirt, he is talking about. Only when the referents designated by the possessive pronouns are made concretely clear to Jonathan by insisting that he touch the shirt he is talking about does he correctly "answer" the question.[12] But is he answering, or is he simply labeling the colors pointed to, which gives the semblance of an answer to a question?

In item 53, my repeating my own question (item 51) may simply be a cue to Jonathan that his previous answer was wrong, stimulating him to switch to another "version" of the answer without really grasping the *rule*, so that, in item 54, he changes only the predicate nominative, not the possessive pronoun. The latter he apparently just echoes. In any event, my own next response, "Right" (item 55), is really crediting him for a wrong answer, i.e., *his* name is not Dr. Churchill. My error.

Formally, the problem here is that pronouns must be reversed: *I, my, mine*, always refer to the speaker, while *you* and *your* always refer to the person spoken to. In other words, the referent is relative rather than absolute. And herein Jonathan encounters an additional complication in dealing with pronouns beyond what *Leon* encountered in dealing with prepositions. So that even in item 80, when Jonathan accurately states, "Your shirt is yellow and blue," there once again is no way to be sure that he is "answering" my question (which implies language competence) rather than just responding by rote and/or echolalia as he names the colors he has most recently touched.

From another perspective, Jonathan tends to avoid dealing with abstract parts of speech by responding only with substantives. His making complete sentences has to be forced. For example, see items 56-60; 66-78. Here, I am programming Jonathan to speak in complete sentences. Left to himself, he would probably respond only with substantives. With comprehension of the

---

[12] In this regard, there is evidence at several points in the transcript that Jonathan may be able to use visual cues to guide appropriate verbalization much better than he can use auditory (and especially *abstract* auditory) cues. While this is not *new* information about Jonathan, it emerges in interesting ways and, again, might remind one of one of *Leon's* pecularities described previously. Aside from this example with the shirts, on three occasions in this interview Jonathan spontaneously and appropriately verbalizes things he sees: (1) Item 116: Jonathan spontaneously and accurately reports that I am pouring apple juice. (2) Items 86 and 88: Jonathan spontaneously and accurately describes two objects which I had introduced, albeit the adjectives "big" and "little" are carryovers from recent training he had had with the concepts of *big* and *little*. (3) Elsewhere in this interview, though not included in the transcript, Jonathan spontaneously and accurately reported, "You are rubbing your eye," something I had been unaware of until Jonathan called my attention to it. Finally, it is of interest that in earlier training sessions with personal pronouns, Jonathan had been taught to make correct distinctions between *I* and *you* by associating these personal pronouns with proper nouns. Thus, he would say, for example, "Jesse, you have . . . ." However, attendant to this "progress" he began confusing the names of people he had known for months, calling them by the wrong name. Again as with *Leon*, one error was corrected, and another introduced. Such is an autistic child's effort to grasp the world through language.

more abstract parts of speech and of syntax lacking, I am probably only teaching echolalia so that at best Jonathan gives only the *appearance* of generating sentences.

We continued this naming of shirt colors until, in item 81, I further complicated things for Jonathan. Here I asked him to contend not only with alternating personal pronouns, but with changing verbs as well. The situation is this: Using two objects which are very familiar to Jonathan, I give him a yellow block while I myself keep a blue cup. Also, Jonathan is sitting down in a chair and I am standing up. The remainder of the transcript, then, is my attempt to get Jonathan to correctly state what he or I *have* (yellow block and blue cup, respectively) or what he or I are *doing* (sitting down and standing up, respectively). Now it is important to note that from past training Jonathan will have no trouble in answering whether he is sitting down or standing up and that he has absolutely no difficulty in naming these two objects (or hundreds of other objects). But the challenge of dealing with a two-way classification, so to speak, guided by discriminative stimuli, leaves him demonstrably incompetent. The task can be formally protrayed like this:

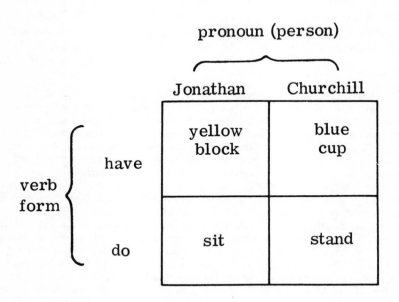

FIG. 19. Jonathan: Diagram of double-classification task.

Now we see that Jonathan has difficulty in responding to a double discrimination. He must say what either *he* or *I* either *have* or are *doing*. In other words, there are four possible questions: (1) What do you have? (2) What do I have? (3) What are you doing? (4) What am I doing?

Just four possible questions. And, under the circumstances, just four possible answers. Simple enough. Surely a child who has memorized "The Night Before Christmas" can remember four short answers to four short questions. But no, he cannot. Cannot because the challenge is not to memory at all but rather to an apprehension of grammatical rules and the two-way classification depicted in Figure 19. Although Jonathan probably could have been conditioned to emit these four "answers" in response to these four "questions," such tricks of training would have brought him no closer to language competence—as all our other training suggests. For the task demands not merely more memory but a leap, as it were, of another order of magnitude. Let's look again at what happened.

What is seen in the ensuing transcript is that Jonathan answers as if he is confusing the pronouns, the auxiliaries, or both. At times (items 99–117, 135–143, 153–163), Jonathan seems to be programmed or drilled into "correct" responses. But as soon as the "set" of the question is changed, he is again in trouble. He is unable to deal with simultaneously varying pronouns and auxiliaries. We seem to be looking at the difference between language performance and language competence.

One strategy which Jonathan adopts appears to be that of establishing a separate "set" for each of us. Following item 119, he appears to deal only with what he is "doing" and with what I "have." Thus, he has himself pegged as *doing* ("sitting in a chair") and he has me pegged as *having* ("a blue cup"). While Jonathan thus lights on two correct responses, this solution appears to preclude recognition that I am also *doing* something ("standing up") and that Jonathan is also *having* something (yellow block). Again, this can be diagrammed. (See Figure 20.)

It is as if two of the cells are nonexistent or irretrievable for Jonathan. Again, this is reminiscent of the cross-referencing problem encountered with other children. Jonathan seems unable to extricate himself from this dilemma. Correct answers are given only after I have given him the correct line to echo (e.g., item 130), but then with the first change in the question, Jonathan is back into the same difficulty. Again, he has to be "programmed" into stating the obvious fact that he is sitting in a chair (see items 131–140).

Elsewhere, we see other strategies, again reminiscent of other children. For instance, when I won't accept his "have" answer, Jonathan gives his "doing" answer (items 150–153). When he thus gets his auxiliaries sorted out, he then displays confusion about pronouns (e.g., item 164). In item 168 he tries to resolve the problem by changing his verb set, giving the "obviously" incorrect

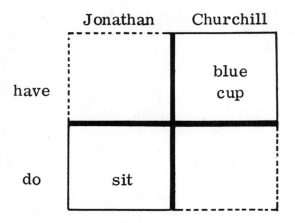

FIG. 20. Jonathan: Diagram of performance on double-classification task.

statement that he is standing up. Or is he attempting to reply that *I* am standing up, and again confusing his pronouns? But in that case he would not be answering the question of item 167, "Jonathan, what do *you* have?" In either case, it is as if he does not recognize where his error lies.

The extent of Jonathan's struggle and frustration is most dramatic when he displays a breakdown concerning substantives. For example, Jonathan reports in item 122 that I have a blue block. There is no blue *block* in the room.

Another example of Jonathan's response to sustained failure is his reaching entirely outside the context of the session for a response. Thus, in item 180 he answers, "I have a forehead." This statement is true. It is also surprising. It is worth recalling that Jonathan had been trained in the past in naming of body parts, including his forehead. Thus, we may infer that this seemingly irrelevant response is probably another example of delayed echolalia.[13] Stumped, Jonathan again calls on his old ally, his excellent rote memory.

There are other strange or quaint answers which Jonathan gives to these four basic questions. For instance, at times he will come up with an apparent absurdity, such as (item 108) when he says, [I am] "a yellow block." However, such a statement is only absurd if it is assumed that the pronoun and verb have semantic value for Jonathan. On the other hand, if these words (actually, sounds) have mere signal value for Jonathan, there is nothing absurd in his

---

[13]Some people might understand Jonathan's reply here to be his way of telling me, "Look, you are asking all these silly questions, and I am giving you silly answers. But I am telling you once and for all that I am not so stupid: I have a forehead!"

incorrect guess as to which substantive to associate with them. Again, his making an error with such an "obvious" fact that he is sitting down, not standing up, is astonishing only if the same assumption is made, i.e., that the pronoun and verb have semantic meaning for him. Assuming to the contrary that these parts of speech have, at most, mere signal value, then the signal value itself is ambiguous. Specifically, the words "I," "you," "my," "your" sometimes refer to Jonathan and sometimes refer to me, and in this context Jonathan is in the position of one who is trying to guess at the outcome of a tossed coin. The semantic meaning of these words is constant (reliable) for one who apprehends the underlying grammatical rule. For one attending only to the surface phenomena (mere sound), pronouns are forever treacherous and best disregarded. In these terms, it is as adaptive for Jonathan to disregard pronouns in answering such questions as it is for me to disregard street noise while writing. Pronouns are in the strict sense *noise* for Jonathan: They contain no information.

Finally, we see in many of Jonathan's responses answers which we must admit are true but which are not pertinent to the question asked. Thus, when he is asked what he is doing and replies, "I have a yellow block" (items 185 and 186), Jonathan has made a true statement, but he has not answered the question. In the context of the transcript at this point, it appears that he has simply not shifted his verb set. When I persist with the same question, Jonathan shifts gears (not only the verb but also the pronoun) and replies, "Dr. Churchill, you are standing up." Another true statement. And again not pertinent to the question asked. Pressed still further with the same question, Jonathan stumbles (item 190) and manages, "Dr. Churchill, you have a bl . block . . (mumble) Ch . you have a blue *cup*," finally stumbling on yet another true statement, but still not answering the question asked. We must wonder eventually whether, even when Jonathan is making statements of fact, he can in any sense be said to be "answering a question." We can examine this more systematically.

In the question and answer format used in this demonstration session, an adequate answer to a question must meet four criteria: (1) The pronoun of the question must be reversed from "you" to "I," or vice versa. (2) The verb of the question must remain the same in the answer, although its form may change. (3) The predicate phrase must be true in relation to its own subject and verb. (4) The answer must be relevant to the question asked. Meeting the first two criteria may be designated colloquially as "getting off on the right foot" in answering the question. Basically, the meeting of these two criteria simply ensures that both parties are talking about the same thing. In everyday discourse, this portion of an answer is commonly omitted since it is understood by both parties and taken for granted. It is in the last two criteria mentioned that the information sought by the question resides. We may ask,

Table 16. Jonathan: Classifiable Responses to Four Questions

Item	Foot			Predicate phrase		
	Pron	Vb	Right?	True?	Relevant?	Adequate
55	x	–	Yes	+	+	Yes
61	x	=	Yes	+?	+	Yes
73	x	–	Yes	√	√	No ←
79	x	=	Yes	+	+	Yes
81	x	–	Yes	+	+	Yes
83	x	–	Yes	+	+	Yes
119	x	=	Yes	+	+	Yes
129	x	=	Yes	√	+	Yes
137	x	=	Yes	√	+	No ←
139	x	=	Yes	+	+	Yes
141	x	=	Yes	+	+	Yes
143	x	=	Yes	+	+	Yes
145	x	=	Yes	+	+	Yes
153	x	=	Yes	√	+	No ←
173b	x	=	Yes	+	+	Yes
179	x	=	Yes	+	√	No ←
183	x	=	Yes	+	+	Yes
97	x	x	No	√	√	No
101	x	x	No	–	–	No
125	x	x	No	√	√	No
167	x	x	No	√	√	No
171	x	x	No	+	√	No
185	x	x	No	+	√	No
51	=	=	No	+	√	No
53	=	=	No	√	√	No
123	=	=	No	+	√	No
131	=	=	No	+	√	No
147	=	=	No	+	√	No
149	=	=	No	+	√	No
173a	=	=	No	√	+	No
187	=	=	No	+	√	No
117	=	x	No	+	√	No
189	=	x	No	+	√	No
197	=	x	No	+	√	No

x means pronoun changed between question and answer; = means verb form is kept constant between question and answer; – means verb elided; + means predicate phrase is true or relevant; √ means predicate phrase is not true or not relevant.

then, whether "getting off on the right foot," i.e., reversing the pronoun and keeping the verb the same as in the question, bears any relation to the adequacy of Jonathan's answer. From the taped transcript, 34 question and answer sequences could be classified according to these four criteria. They are displayed in Table 16. (Other verbal interactions include such things as interruptions, incomplete phrases, and the training of echolalic responses, which are not amenable to this classification.)

Assuming a complete answer, there are four possible pronoun-verb combinations, only one of which represents starting off on the right foot. Jonathan did so on 17, or exactly half, of these 34 answers. On 14 of these answers (82%), the ensuing predicate phrase was adequate, i.e., it was *both* a true statement *and* was relevant to the question asked. In contrast, it is seen that Jonathan's answer (predicate phrase) was never adequate if, in any way, he started off on the "wrong foot."

Looking at those predicate phrases which are not adequate, the commonest type of error (57% of errors) might be described as an "irrelevant truth." That is, Jonathan makes a statement which is true at face value, but which does not answer the question asked. On three occasions, his answer is relevant to the question asked, but simply wrong. On five occasions, his answer is not relevant to the question asked nor would it be true in any event. Once, there was simply no predicate phrase response.

Thus, it appears that starting on the "right foot" may be important if Jonathan is to respond to a simple question with adequate information. However, it cannot be concluded even then that this is any more than a surface phenomenon, i.e., we cannot infer "understanding" of the question from this. If anything, the preponderance of errors of the "irrelevant truth" type might be used to argue that Jonathan does not understand even simple questions but simply tries to match auditory stimuli as best he can from a sizeable repertoire of conditioned vocal responses.

Looking at Jonathan's performance in this way raises some training issues. For instance, should he always have been interrupted when he started out on the "wrong foot" in answer to a question, i.e., when he did not reverse the pronoun and keep the verb constant? On two or three occasions, it was seen that my own confusion, or at least inconsistency, in giving feedback to Jonathan about the correctness/incorrectness of his answers could have added to his own confusion. As another dilemma, should "irrelevant facts" be ignored, rewarded, labeled as incorrect, or what? To some degree the proper training approach would depend on whether the objective is to shape speech or to inculcate grammatical rules. On the one hand, it seems clear that mere speech-shaping, however protracted, can never lead to language competence; on the other hand, I know of no evidence that syntactical rules ("deep structure"?) can be taught—they seem to be spontaneously apprehended by the young child exposed to any language whatever.

Table 17. Articulation

	Poor articulation	Unintelligible where one would expect a . . .	Elisions
Pronoun	9	4	1
Verb	12	5	5
Proper noun	2	–	–
Color?/Article?	1	–	–
Unknown		5	

Although Jonathan's articulation and volume are generally very good, this is not always the case. Occasionally, his articulation becomes ambiguous, or he is even unintelligible. Such points are marked in the transcript by asterisks. It is noteworthy that his poor articulation occurs selectively. As might be expected, it is almost entirely confined to pronoun and verb forms, i.e., to those parts of speech with which he here has the most difficulty. Jonathan is never unintelligible when uttering substantives. On six occasions, he is found to elide a word altogether: five times where one would expect a verb, once where a pronoun. Since he also occasionally uses contracted forms of pronoun-verb, e.g., "I'm" and "you're," a claim that these elisions represent some "difficulty" with language seems unwarranted. They may well represent a normal phenomenon in language development. Nevertheless, the almost exclusive occurrence of poor articulation with pronouns and verbs is striking. Furthermore, the transcript includes 14 occasions of unintelligible communication, and 9 of these 14 unintelligible utterances occur where one would expect either a pronoun or a verb to occur. Since Jonathan has absolutely no articulation problem and sometimes utters the words in question loud and clear, it is tempting to infer that his articulation becomes poor or even unintelligible when he literally doesn't know what to say—and in some sense *knows* that he doesn't know. Table 17 presents that articulation data in summary form.

One final sidelight on Jonathan's speech: A continuous record of Jonathan's speech was made from 8:00 a.m. until 3:30 p.m. in a single day. All of his utterances in the course of this routine day were tape recorded and transcribed. This included structured training sessions, free play, small group activities, meals, etc. His speech was then classified as spontaneous utterances, immediate echolalia, delayed echolalia, and answers to questions. The classification was made by a person who had observed Jonathan throughout the 7½ hours of the recording and who did not know the purpose to which

Table 18. Jonathan: Day-Long Speech Corpus

	Categories of speech			
	Spontaneous utterances (SU)	Delayed echolalia (DE)	Answers to questions (AQ)	Immediate echolalia (IE)
n	26	40	107	24
Percent of total utterances	13	20	54	12
Mean words per category	2.08	3.22	3.84	4.58

One-way analysis of variance

Source	df	SS	MS
Between	3	106.8	35.60
Within	193	548.7	2.84
Total	196	655.5	

$F = 12.54$, $df = 3$ and 193, $p < .001$.

Special comparisons*

Categories being compared	Observed difference	Number of means in this range	Difference necessary for significance (Q_p) $(S_{\bar{x}})$	Yardstick	Conclusions
SU × IE	2.50	4	(4.50) (.337)	1.52	$p < .01$
SU × AQ	1.76	3	(4.20) (.2074)	.87	$p < .01$
IE × DE	1.36	3			
SU × DE	1.14	2	(2.80) (.2074)	.58	$p < .05$
AQ × IE	0.74	2			
DE × AQ	0.62	2			

*Neuman-Keuls test for the Studentized range.

the classification would be put. Excluding a few unintelligible (usually inaudible) utterances, Jonathan spoke 197 classifiable words, phrases or sentences in this time. These were examined in terms of number of words per phrase or sentence and analyzed using a one-way analysis of variance.

As seen, one half of what Jonathan had to say in the course of this day was in response to questions, which in turn occurred mostly during training sessions. Another way of saying this is that without such "prodding"—for better or for worse—Jonathan's total verbal output world be reduced by over one-half, a point not unnoticed by those who view the silence of autistic children as a matter of faulty conditioning. What might be considered delayed echolalia comprised less than a quarter of his utterances, while another quarter was evenly divided between what was clearly immediate echolalia and what appeared to be Jonathan's very own, spontaneously generated, expressions and comments on the world. The upper part of Table 18 rank orders the categories of speech according to mean number of words per category. Length of utterance has been said to reflect both developmental levels and intelligence. Children normally speak in two-word phrases around age 2, and about age 3 are speaking three words at a time. Jonathan, we see, in his spontaneous utterances, had a mean phrase length of just two words. The longest string of words usually occur in immediate imitation of what he has just heard. Analysis indicates a statistically significant difference between each of the means as if they were drawn from truly different categories of speech. Since Jonathan was thought of as such a verbal child, it is of especial interest that his spontaneous utterances resemble, in length of phrase, those of a 2-year-old child. So from still another direction, the evidence suggests that Jonathan's ability with language is less than it seems.

In conclusion, then, Jonathan displayed easy mastery of the lower reaches of the 9WL and appeared to have the skills requisite for fully functional speech. Yet a detailed and systematic look at Jonathan's speech when even the simplest demands are made for competence with syntax shows, from several directions, a severe language disability. Some aspects of his performance closely resemble what is observed in much lower functioning autistic children, while other aspects seem more unique to more verbal children such as Leon. His difficulty with what is here described as two-way classification may be crucial and would seem to impose, even without any other impediments, a severe limitation on his ability to develop functional language. Again we see some preferential use of visual rather than auditory discriminative stimuli. And again we see evidence of an intelligent, patterned effort to cope with a task, as well as some awareness of the point at which the task is too much for him.

ORSON

Orson was a physically attractive blond child who often seemed sullen and negativistic. His speech was well articulated, and he was able to generate and understand short novel sentences. He had had previous experience in a Montessori school but had been excluded because of his behavior. He was 5 years and 1 month of age at the midpoint of testing with the 9WL. He completed all tasks, including generalization and cross-referencing tasks, during 52 sessions in less than 5 weeks. When evaluated by us and diagnosed as an autistic child, his relationships were often stormy, hostile, and negative. His WISC IQ scores were as follows: Performance 115, Verbal 72, Full Scale 92. On follow-up at age 7 years and 5 months, these scores were 111, 80, and 94, respectively, and he was given the same social rating as before, 2.

Orson's performance on the 9WL was superlative with one or two exceptions. He learned tasks with minimal training and made practically no

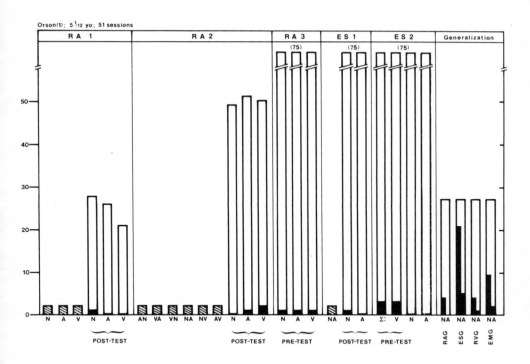

FIG. 21. Orson's histogram (1). (For legend, see Figs. 2 and 5.)

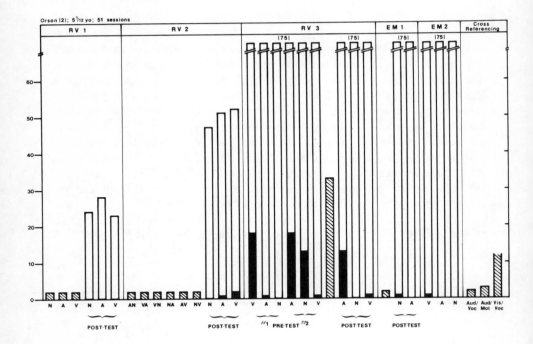

FIG. 22. Orson's histogram (2). (For legend, see Figs. 2 and 5.)

errors on any pre-tests or post-tests. In other words, he promptly demonstrated mastery of all parts of speech and the functional receptive and expressive modalities. The single exception—and it was a relatively minor obstacle considering other autistic children—occurred on the RV3 task. This represents the only part of the 9WL where Orson stumbled. Whereas in all other tasks he had reached criterion in the minimum time of 2 training sessions, he required 36 blocks of 25 trials (12 training sessions) on the RV3 task before reaching criterion.

The source of his difficulty is suggested on examining the two RV3 pre-tests and the RV3 post-test in Figure 22. On all of these, it is seen that his errors display a sequence effect, i.e., given a 3-word stimulus, any error was likely to occur on the first word of the 3-word stimulus. Thus, on the first pre-test, when the stimulus sequence was verb-adjective-noun, he made 18 verb errors, only 1 adjective error, and no noun errors. Immediately following, when the sequence was switched to adjective-noun-verb, he made 18 adjective errors, 13 noun errors, and only 1 verb error. After the 12 training sessions, on a post-test employing adjective-noun-verb sequence, he made 13 adjective errors, no noun errors, and a single verb error. This suggests that Orson's only difficulty in handling a 3-word sentence, visually presented, was related to a memory factor, or perhaps to the number of "bits" of information that he could handle at once. As there had been no hint of a sequence effect on the RV2 task, it may be inferred that passing from 2 to 3 bits of visual information exceeded Orson's memory/complexity threshold at this particular stage of development. This appeared, however, to be only a limitation of "capacity," and there was no other indication from the 9WL that Orson suffered any disability with respect to receptive or expressive modalities or in handling particular parts of speech.

Closer inspection of Orson's 12 training sessions on the RV3 task holds some interest. During this time—his first frustration with the 9WL—Orson vacillated between withdrawal, anxious asking if he were "right," rather random or chaotic error patterns, and finally, just prior to final mastery of the task, a definite error pattern. Throughout this training period the stimulus sequence was held constant: adjective-noun-verb. During the first 3 sessions, his total errors as well as "no responses" increased, whereupon for the next 5 sessions the verb was kept the same in each block of 25 trials, and only the adjective and noun were varied. Thereafter, he reached criterion while verbs as well as adjectives and nouns were varied. The adjective-noun-verb sequence was maintained throughout. In all training sessions except three (his third, fourth, and penultimate) Orson made two to three times more errors on adjectives than on nouns. The penultimate session, when mixed verbs were reintroduced, resulted in more verb than adjective or noun errors. Finally, as already noted, the post-test resulted in 14 element errors out of a total of 225, with all but one of these occurring on the first element, adjectives.

On EM1, Orson had absolutely no difficulty in mastering the task, but some curious things emerged in his response pattern. In this task, the child is shown one of the nine objects of the 9WL. He must respond with the hand sign which correctly designates the color or the shape or both color and shape of the stimulus object. Initially, if a stick or ring of any color were presented, Orson consistently gave the correct sign for the shape of the object; he never gave the color sign. If a blue or yellow block were presented, he consistently gave the correct sign for the color of the object; he never gave the shape sign. If a red block were presented, he always gave the correct sign for both color and shape. However, early in the post-test, he began responding to the red block stimulus with the correct sign for the color only, so that sticks and rings of any color regularly elicited a shape sign, while blocks of any color regularly elicited a color sign. This way of organizing his possible responses may have carried over into the EMG test which was given immediately after the EM1 sequence: He missed the block stimulus in each of the nine sets of objects, responding in each case with a red, blue, or yellow color sign even though, by test design, none of the block stimuli were now red or blue or yellow. It is as if his "theory" of how the world is would run something like this: "If it's a block, give a color response; if it's a ring or a stick, give a shape response." Orson was absolutely consistent in adhering to this "theory" even when it led to errors and negative feedback.[14] Yet immediately before and after the EMG test, the "block" hand sign response was clearly within Orson's response repertoire. Also on the EMG test, he made only two adjective errors, i.e., presented with a red, blue, or yellow object which was not shaped like a block, stick, or ring he gave a correct color response to 25 out of 27 novel stimulus objects.

On other generalization tests, Orson showed little difficulty except on ESG (see Fig. 21). Here, Orson responded with incorrect vocalizations almost 50% of the time. Once again, however, these errors seem to represent a shortcoming of the test or an incorrect response set on Orson's part: 21 of 26 errors occurred in response to a "color" stimulus, and usually Orson correctly named the object involved ("ribbon," "shoe," etc.). Toward the end of this test, he tended to switch to the correct color response after not being rewarded for correctly naming the object.

Orson was trained in three cross-referencing tasks (see Fig. 22). On the first, he was shown one of the 9WL objects together with an auditory discriminative stimulus, i.e., the word "color" or "object," and he was required to say the correct word (auditory-vocal association). He reached criterion in minimum time. The second cross-referencing task was the same, except that the response was required in hand signs (auditory-motor association). He reached criterion almost as soon. The next four sessions, which ended Orson's work with the 9WL objects, were again a cross-referencing task in which the discrminative stimulus was presented visually: Together with one of the nine objects, a 3 X 5 card showing either a star or a helix shape was presented to indicate whether a correct color or shape response, respectively, would be reinforced. The response was again vocal. In 12 blocks of 25 trials, Orson never reached criterion, but after his first session he always ranged between 18–20 correct responses in 25 trials. Thus, it is likely that had training continued Orson would have shortly reached criterion on this task as well. Once again, training/testing was interrupted by clinical considerations not pertinent to the present subject, and further study of Orson's language was not pursued.

---

[14] As already described, a similar "strategy" was employed at times by *Leon* and by *Jonathan*. Of course, such a response pattern may not be unique to autistic children, and the matter cannot be settled through the present design.

CURTIS

Curtis was 6 years and 4 months of age when he worked with the 9WL. In 44 sessions covering less than a month, Curtis covered the entire 9WL including the 4 generalization tests and the four cross-referencing tasks. Curtis was an attractive blond child who had been diagnosed as autistic. His Vineland Social Quotient was 74. On the Peabody Picture Vocabulary, his IQ was 34. On the Cattell-Binet test, his IQ was 45. He was generally quite shy and timid and had a social rating of 3. At follow-up, 25 months later, he was given a WISC, which yielded a Performance IQ 110, Verbal IQ 53, Full Scale IQ 78. Despite his low verbal score, he was doing quite well socially and at the time of the follow-up did not stand out to his teachers as being different than most children of his age.

Curtis' performance on the 9WL is the best of any child who had been diagnosed autistic and is comparable to that of a normal or mildly retarded

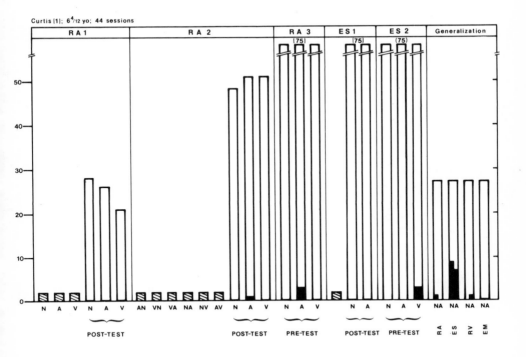

FIG. 23. Curtis' histogram (1). (For legend, see Figs. 2 and 5.)

Curtis (2): 6 ^{4}/12 yo; 44 sessions

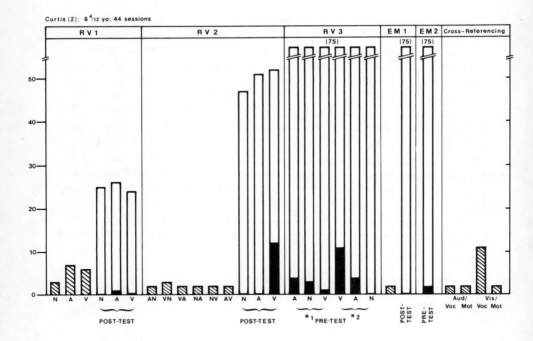

FIG. 24. Curtis' histogram (2). (For legend, see Figs. 2 and 5.)

child without specific sensory, perceptual, or linguistic problems. In viewing Figure 23, it is seen that Curtis mastered all receptive auditory and expressive vocal tasks with minimum training and that he made only 1 error on 3 different post-tests (375 test trials in all). Indeed, he performed so well that on the RA3 and ES2 tasks he was pre-tested and, because on each of these tests he made only 3 errors in 225 trials, no further training was given on these tasks. On the RV1 task, Curtis did require a little more training before reaching criterion, but on post-tests he made only 1 error in 75 trials. On RV2 he reached criterion with minimum training on five of the six 2-word combinations. He made 12 errors in 150 trials on the RV2 post-test. All of these errors occurred on the verb element, and nine of them occurred when the verb was the first element of the 2-word stimulus. It is not clear whether these verb errors represent some difficulty in translating visual information into a motor act, but in any event the occurrence of 75% of these errors when the verb was the first element of the 2-word stimulus again points to a sequence effect. This is congruent with the observation that during the training period Curtis failed to reach criterion in minimum time only when a verb was first presented as the first element of the 2-word stimulus (VN).

Performance on RV3 suggests that the sequence effect is prepotent over any special weakness with verbs per se. On this task he was given two pre-tests with the elements of speech arranged differently on each test (ANV and VAN, respectively). On both occasions a sequence effect was seen, and the fact that he made the most errors on pre-test #2 (11 verb errors when verbs were in the first position: VAN sequence) suggests that there may have been some additive effect which combined part of speech and sequence to produce the highest number of errors at this point. However, this was a relatively minor difficulty, since Curtis still made 84% correct responses even at his worst. On EM1, Curtis again reached criterion with minimum training and made no errors on post-test. An EM2 pre-test was given on which he made only two errors, so further training on this test was not done.

On the four generalization tests, Curtis made either no errors or 1 error in 54 trials on 3 of the 4 tests (see Fig. 23). Only on the expressive speech generalization (ESG) did he show more errors. Examining this test more closely shows that his 16 errors here (9 noun, 7 adjective errors) are of the same type as those made by other autistic children who are verbal, for Curtis scored "errors" by appropriately naming the object presented rather than staying within the "set" of the 9WL. In addition, the test was irregularly administered since an initial series of six familiarization trials with 9WL objects was omitted.

Finally, on the cross-referencing tasks, Curtis displayed no difficulty making correct vocal or motor responses when the discriminative stimulus was auditory (see Fig. 24). When first presented with a visual discriminative stimulus [cards displaying either a star (color) or a helix (object)], he did require 11 blocks of 24 trials before reaching criterion. Immediately after, using the same discriminative stimuli, Curtis reached criterion on motor responses in minimum time.

In summary, Curtis represents a child who showed very little difficulty, even temporarily, in progressing all the way through the 9WL tasks. He was tested with the 9WL during the early period of its use. At that time, we were primarily interested in comparing the performances on the 9WL of as many children as possible—a long and tedious process with each. Consequently—and unfortunately—Curtis was not examined concerning higher levels of language organization.

EDGAR

Edgar was 5½ years of age at the midpoint of testing with the 9WL. Diagnosed as an autistic child, his Vineland Social Quotient was 84. On the

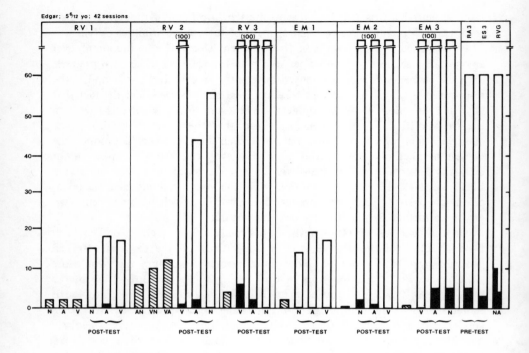

FIG. 25. Edgar's histogram. (For legend, see Figs. 2 and 5.)

Peabody Picture Vocabulary he had a verbal IQ of 76. His Stanford-Binet IQ was 74. He was given a social rating of 1, which includes children who are clinging and dependent, possibly showing less inhibition in relating to strangers than one might expect for a child of that age. On follow-up at age 8 and 5 months, however, his social rating was given a 4, indicating that at that time he was considered a loner, often seemed lost in his own world, and only people who knew him well could occasionally gain his attention or acceptance. Nevertheless, on the WISC at that time, his Performance IQ was 107, Verbal IQ was 64, and Full Scale IQ was 83. In light of this great discrepancy between performance and verbal scores, Edgar's 9WL histogram (Fig. 25) holds some interest for it shows a very low profile, i.e., Edgar required little training to reach criterion on various tasks, and on the various post-tests he made few errors. This suggests that the basic conditionability or one-to-one associations, which are necessary as a substrate for language competence, were present in Edgar and that his later poor performance on the WISC verbal scales is a reflection of some higher deficit. The same might well be said of *Curtis*.

Edgar was another child who was trained and tested early in the development of the 9WL. Again his training trails were scored only as correct/incorrect and cannot be analyzed individually for error patterns and learning strategies. Also, he did not proceed as systematically through the entire 9WL as did children at a later date. Being a child with rather good language to begin with, only the receptive visual and expressive motor portions of the test were given completely. Receptive auditory and expressive speech tasks were not presented at their simplest, lowest levels; instead, RA3 and ES3 post-tests were immediately given with essentially no training on these tasks. Of the generalization tests, only the RVG had been designed at that time, and the cross-referencing task had not yet been devised. In all, Edgar had 42 training and testing sessions. As can be seen in Figure 25, Edgar reached criterion on the RV1 task in minimum time and on the post-test made only one error (adjective). He required a bit more training on the RV2 task, but on the post-test he made only 3 errors in 100 trials. Four blocks of 25 trials were sufficient for Edgar to reach criterion on the RV3 task, and, once again, his errors on the post-test were few. The gradient across parts of speech is reminiscent of a sequence effect seen in other children, but there were really too few errors to state this with much certainty. Moving to the expressive motor tasks, Edgar again reached criterion in minimum time, and on the post-test he made no errors. He had essentially no training before the EM2 and EM3 post-tests, on both of which he made few errors. It is curious that while on the RV3 post-test he made most errors on the first part of the 3-word stimulus, on the EM3 post-test he made no errors on this part and made equal numbers of errors on the seond and third parts of speech. Perhaps this can be attributed to the differing stimuli in the two tests: On the RV3 post-test he was required to make a differential response on the basis of discriminating rather similar hand signs; on the EM3 post-test, he observed the behavior of the adult with the 9WL objects and "described" this behavior with the appropriate hand signs. It may well be that observing another person *slide*, *tap*, or *give* an object is more dramatically different (and more memorable?) than is the counterpart of simply observing another person make hand signs for these actions.

Although receiving no training prior to the RA3 and ES3 tests, he made over 90% correct responses on both occasions. This was not surprising to us—indeed, it was our initial reason for omitting training to criterion. The RVG reflects a higher percentage of errors, but still a 72% rate of correct responding. The familiar pattern of more noun than adjective errors on this particular task probably reflects once again the bias of the test rather than a particular deficit in Edgar.

EDWARD

Edward was 5 years and 7 months of age at the midpoint of testing with the 9WL. He had been diagnosed as a high autistic child. On the Vineland, his Social Quotient was 74. Peabody Picture Vocabulary IQ was 57. On the Stanford-Binet his IQ was 62. Socially he was given a rating of 4, indicating that he was generally a loner and often seemed lost in his own world, although those who knew him well could get his attention or acceptance at times. Edward was a professor's child, a very pretty, brown-haired, wide-eyed boy with a generally sweet disposition. Although occasionally he would talk when emotionally excited, for the most part he seemed very quiet and retiring. He was not particularly obsessive or ritualistic—he was simply a very retiring, shadowy, soft child. On follow-up at age 10 years 3 months, Edward's WISC Performance IQ was 72. On the ITPA his verbal quotient was 55. Socially, he was still given a rating of 4.

Edward was another of the first children to be trained and tested with the 9WL, and, except for some of the post-tests, recording was not done trial by trial. Therefore, close examination of error patterns and learning strategies is impossible; only some overall statements can be made about Edward's performance in being trained to criterion. Also, only the receptive visual portions of the 9WL were given (see Fig. 26). These were completed in 39 sessions. The limited use of the 9WL with Edward was due largely to the lack of appreciation at that time for the value of systematically checking out all modalities even with a child like Edward who had very good speech *when* he chose to talk.

On RV1 tasks, Edward was trained initially with nouns, using only two objects at first. In spite of such a simple start, and in spite of behavioral indications of both cooperativeness and good motivation in Edward, he did not reach criterion until the equivalent of 43 blocks of 25 trials (1,075 training trials). While Edward's individual responses cannot now be recovered, his overall scores show a low level of correct responses (25–50%) until just two sessions before he reached criterion. Then, in two sessions, he jumped to 100% correct responding on nouns, where he essentially remained ever after. The story is much the same when he next was trained on adjectives. A rather protracted period of a low level of correct responding culminated in a rapid climb to consistent, 100% correct responding. There was a procedural blunder in training Edward on verbs, so that he did not have a chance to reach criterion. However, by the fifth block of 25 trials he had already achieved a high level of correct responding, and on post-test he made no errors on nouns, adjectives, or verbs although on 2 of the 50 trials he did fail on respond.

On the RV2 tasks, Edward was trained using only three 2-word combinations. On all three, he reached criterion within 8 or 9 blocks of 25

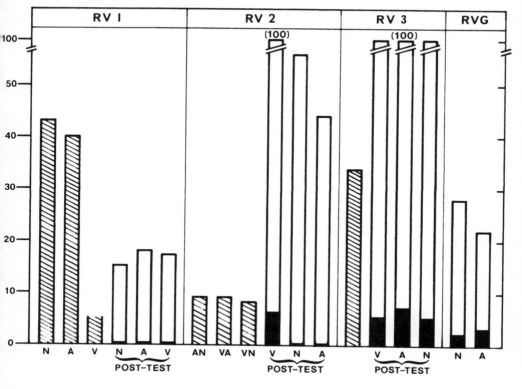

FIG. 26. Edward's histogram. (For legend, see Figs. 2 and 5.)

trials, usually with the help of having one of the parameters limited initially. We now have no opportunity to see whether Edward's errors displayed a sequence effect, but the post-test suggests that this might have been. The post-test in this case consisted of a randomly chosen verb hand sign followed by a randomly chosen noun or adjective sign, with 100 trials in all. Thus, the verb, which represented the stimulus most distant from Edward's response, was the element on which he made six errors, while he made no errors on the more proximal noun or adjective stimuli. Of course, on the RV1 task Edward had had much less training on verbs than on either nouns or adjectives, and this might also be a factor in his missing only verbs on the RV2 post-test.

When presented with the RV3 task, Edward made a higher number of correct responses from the beginning (about 75%), but he did not reach criterion until after the equivalent of 34 blocks of 25 trials. The post-test once again consisted of 100 randomized trials, the elements being sequenced verb-adjective-noun. The errors were few, and rather evenly distributed across all parts of speech, as shown in Figure 26.

Lastly, a receptive visual generalization test was given (again, different from the more "standard" test used later), and in 50 trials Edward made 2 errors in response to a noun visual stimulus, and 3 in response to an adjective.

Since all training session responses were recorded only as correct or incorrect, we cannot further scrutinize Edward's performance. Nevertheless, it was surprising that this bright-eyed, verbal but very shy child took so long to meet criterion on RV1. He seemed to be a "slow starter," but once he "caught on," he performed very consistently and with a high rate of success.

BETSY

Betsy was 7 years and 1 month of age at the midpoint of work with the 9WL. She had 111 training and testing sessions over a period of 3 months. She had been diagnosed as a high-functioning autistic child. While her Draw-A-Person test indicated an IQ of 81, on the Peabody Picture Vocabulary test her IQ was 37. Her social rating was 4, ascribed to children who "often seem lost in their own world; generally a loner; people who know the child well can get the child's attention or acceptance at times." No follow-up information is available. Betsy was one of the more verbal children on the research unit, but her behavior and speech were particularly disorganized, so that when she was not quietly withdrawn she tended to attract attention because of bizarre and flagrantly inappropriate behavior.

On the RA1 task, Betsy reached criterion almost with minimum training. The post-test reveals only 4 errors in 75 randomized trials, and all 3 of her noun errors involved an "uncalled for" response (tapping an object in response to only a noun stimulus). In addition, there were also six no-response type errors: two following a noun stimulus, three following an adjective, and one following a verb. No other child had displayed this nonresponding on a just-mastered task. Thus, even at the simplest level of the 9WL, Betsy already displayed some unusual response features, redundant responding as well nonresponding.

On the RA2 task, Betsy was pre-tested, and in 75 trials she made only 1 adjective and 1 verb error while there were 5 no-responses. All of the nonresponding occurred in the last block of 25 trials. During subsequent training on the RA2 task, Betsy reached criterion for all six 2-word combinations almost in minimum time. However, her pattern of nonresponding persisted. Over 11 sessions on the RA2 task (825 trials), her errors were distributed as follows: nouns, 13; adjectives, 13; verbs, 8; no-response, 101. Furthermore, in every session her nonresponding increased progressively through each block of 25 trials. No sequence effect was evident on the 2-word task. On the RA2 post-test, while making only 3 errors in 75 trials (one for each part of speech), there were again 7 no-responses.

A possible sequence effect first appeared on the RA3 pre-test, suggesting that Betsy's performance might have been related to the number of bits of information which had been remembered.[15] Also, the nonresponding increased: 2, 3, and 9 no-responses on the 3 blocks of 25 trials. During RA3 training, the adjective-noun-verb sequence was maintained, but the final element of the stimulus, the verb, was fixed. When no improvement was seen in two sessions, the noun as well as the verb was kept constant. In other words, the only varying

[15]The sequence effect on RA3 is really presumptive, since we did not reverse the sequence of stimulus elements to demonstrate the highest number of errors would remain on the distal stimulus element regardless of which part of speech was presented there.

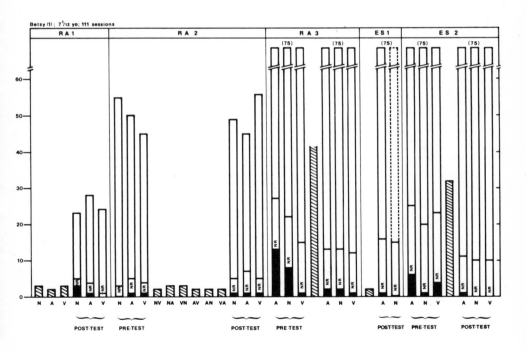

FIG. 27. Betsy's histogram (1). (For legend, see Figs. 2 and 5.)

element in the 3-word stimulus was now the adjective. For a while, Betsy began making more errors on the fixed elements! By varying which elements of the stimulus were fixed, Betsy's errors decreased. However, she continued to miss more first-element stimuli (adjectives) and her level of nonresponding remained high, often exceeding the number of actual errors made. Training was terminated at the pre-set point of 14 training sessions (42 blocks of 25 trials) despite the fact that Betsy had not quite reached criterion. On the RA3 post-test, she made only five errors although there was again a significant level of nonresponding.

On the ES1 task, Betsy reached criterion in minimum time and made a single error on the post-test although she failed to respond 15 times. All of her responses were adjectives. Later, following the RA3 task, the ES2 task was presented. Although there were only 11 errors on ES2 pre-test, Betsy failed to respond 19 times. During the training sessions which followed, she did not reach criterion until 32 blocks of 25 trials. The data show that there were only 5 to 10 errors per 75 trials, but nonresponding soared to 50–75 trials per session. A correction procedure seemed not to influence this, so 3-minute time-outs following five consecutive failures to respond was introduced. Subsequently, the nonresponding began to drop again to previous levels. By the time criterion was reached in the training sessions, Betsy was making only a few adjective errors. On a post-test of 75 randomized trials, she made a single adjective error (in 75 trials) while failing to respond on 10 other trials. Interestingly, Betsy responded with all three parts of speech on each occasion that she responded at all.

When presented next with the RV1 task, Betsy immediately displayed more difficulty than at any previous point on the 9WL. She reached criterion on nouns alone only after 36 blocks of 25 trials, and most of this training could be accomplished only in minute steps by presenting only two different objects at a time, e.g., a red block and a red ring. She did, however, finally reach criterion on nouns alone using a full stimulus array of nine objects. (See Figure 28.) Adjectives, however, were even more difficult for her, and she had not even progressed beyond discriminating two colors at a time, e.g., red stick and yellow stick, when she reached the pre-set training limit of 42 blocks of 25 trials (1,050 trials). At that point, training with adjectives was discontinued. She reached criterion on verbs quickest (19 blocks of 25 trials), possibly because the hand signs for verbs are more suggestive of the response to be made. On the RV1 post-test, Betsy made only 39 correct responses in 75 trials—barely half correct. In spite of this poor performance, there was no nonresponding. The distribution of post-test errors shown on the histogram mirrors the speed with which she reached criterion on the three words during the training sessions. Thus, we see that fewer than a quarter of her responses to adjective stimuli were correct, no better than chance. Also evident on the RV1 post-test is a tendency of Betsy to "over respond," i.e., she included in

Betsy (2); 7 $^1/_{12}$ yo; **111 sessions**

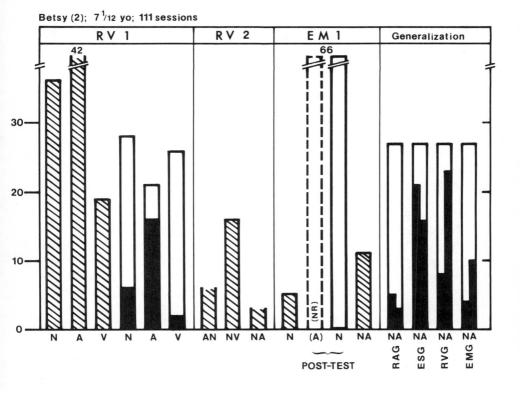

FIG. 28. Betsy's histogram (2). (For legend, see Figs. 2 and 5.)

her response verb elements which were not present in the stimulus: On 25 occasions she included in her response an uncalled for verb response, 24 of these uncalled for responses being *tap*. It was as if she "read in" more than was there.

When presented next with the EM1 task, Betsy reached criterion in 5 blocks of 25 trials, establishing during this process an exclusive noun response set. On the post-test she made 75 errorless noun responses, and again, curiously, there was no nonresponding. She was then given four additional EM1 sessions in which an adjective response was prompted. At best, she came to include 38 unprompted adjective responses in 75 trials, 30 of which (79%) were correct responses to the stimulus object. Although this reflects significant improvement in correct responding to color stimuli as compared to what she had demonstrated on the RV1 task, it is not clear whether the improvement is related to further practice in labelling colors, the use of a different primary modality (expressive motor rather than receptive visual), or other unrecognized factors.

Betsy's work with the 9WL ended with the next task, RV2, which was never completed because of her discharge from the hospital. She was presented only three of the 2-word combinations and, as presaged by her performance on RV1, encountered difficulty. In two adjective-plus-noun sessions she responded correctly less than a third of the time, and all but 4 of her 106 errors were adjective errors. It is unclear whether this was a sequence effect or related to the part of speech; but her later performance on the noun-plus-adjective sequence would suggest that both factors were involved, for in that single session she again made correct responses just a third of the time and her errors included 6 nouns (first element) and 17 adjectives (second or proximal element). The rest of the errors were scored because of prompts. She did do better on the noun-plus-verb sequence, reaching criterion after 16 blocks of 25 trials. Here, she was working with the two parts of speech where she had previously demonstrated mastery on RV1. Over 6 noun-plus-verb sessions, she made 90 noun errors and 32 verb errors. Again this must be construed as representing either a sequence effect, a part of speech effect (possibly reflecting RV1), or both. As Betsy's work with the 9WL was terminated at this point, it was not possible to further elucidate these relationships.

There was a familiar transition as Betsy mastered the noun-plus-verb task: When her previously high rate of noun errors dropped, her previously low rate of verb errors rose just prior to her mastery of the task. This is depicted in Figure 29.

Of particular interest with Betsy are the generalization tests (sessions 8, 12, 92, 101). On the RAG, Betsy did quite well, making only five noun errors and three adjective errors. However, she did poorly on the ESG, making errors on more than two-thirds of her responses. As with other children who have rather good ability to name objects and seem to do poorly on the ESG because of giving "too good" responses, Betsy scored many of her errors through leaving the response set demanded by the task.[16] She again did poorly on the RVG, in particular missing almost all adjectives. However, she followed this one week later with a remarkably good performance on the EMG, making 74% correct responses.

Betsy presented some unique features in her work with the 9WL. For one thing, she had a higher rate of nonresponding than any other child, and this

---

[16]Generalization tests are preceded by a familiarization/review session and the first six trials of each test is with the 9WL objects. On these, Betsy scored 6/6, 5/6, 5/6, 6/6, respectively.

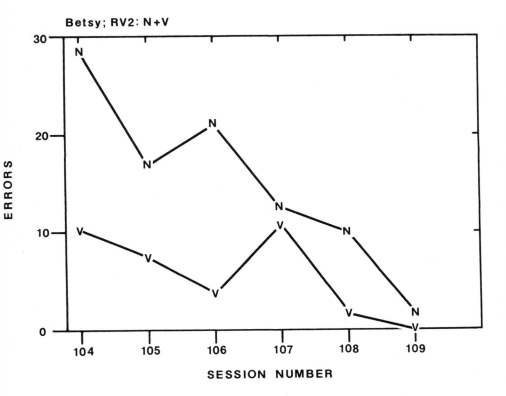

FIG. 29. Betsy: Receptive Visual 2-word task (RV2), noun plus verb.

increased in each block in each session. But it was observed only on receptive auditory and expressive speech tasks—which did not appear to be the most difficult parts of the 9WL for Betsy. One might impute boredom, but behavioral notes do not support that. On RA3 (ANV sequence) when the verb (or noun and verb) was fixed, Betsy began to miss *fixed* parts even though on the pre-test her errors had been almost exclusively on adjectives. However, overall on the RA and ES tasks she did fairly well. In contrast, she had great difficulty on the RV tasks. This, plus her unusual performance on generalization tests, suggest that her receptive visual and expressive vocal modalities were especially deficient, while her receptive auditory and expressive motor modalities were relatively intact. Now, in these children it appears that the receptive auditory and expressive vocal functions are rather highly correlated, as are the receptive visual and expressive motor functions.

Deficiencies tended to show up in these *paired* functions. But in Betsy there was some implication of only one-half of each of these pairs being selectively but seriously deficient—it was as if she could receive sounds but not speak, could execute motor acts but not see! If so, this might help explain the smattering of widely fragmented abilities in Betsy, none of which seems to fit together but which gives the appearance to the casual observer of many abilities but also of unusual disorganization.

Betsy stood out among the other children as being unusually "crazy." In other respects, some of her error patterns and learning strategies seemed to be those seen in other autistic children, e.g., sequence effect and the replacement of old error patterns with new ones before task mastery. She also tended to "over respond," i.e., she included in her response some elements which were not present in the stimulus.

The next three children to be described were not autistic.

STEVE

Steve was 4 years and 11 months of age at the time of testing with the 9WL. He had been diagnosed as an aphasic, mildly retarded child and had manifested none of the characteristics of autism. His Vineland Social Quotient was 70; Verbal Quotient was 33. On the Cattell-Binet Test, his IQ was 34. His social rating was 4, i.e., he related rather well to people he knew, but otherwise was a "loner." Nevertheless, he was not self-absorbed or ritualistic. Such speech as he had was appropriate, as was his play. However, both speech and play were immature for his age. On follow-up at 6 years and 8 months of age, he achieved a social rating of 0, i.e., he seemed socially no different than most children his age. At the time, his WISC Performance IQ was 86, Verbal IQ 65, Full Scale IQ 72. Steve had 95 sessions in a little more than 2 months. This actually represents about twice the number of sessions which would have been required had Steve been led through the protocol as expeditiously as possible.

Steve's performance on the 9WL tasks is of special interest because he was diagnostically different than most of the other children who were tested. He was an easy child to work with. A glance at his histograms shows that with rare exception he met criterion on all tasks in minimum time, and on both pre-test and post-tests his errors were very rare. On most such occasions, he displayed errorless performance across hundreds of trials. Such a histogram is one which we believe characterizes a child with no inherent language disability—at least from the standpoint of basic conditionability: Tasks of carefully arranged, increasing difficulty are learned rather quickly, and insurmountable learning/teaching problems are not encountered; once learned, performance is accurate and reliable over many trials. It is this kind of performance which we expect in normal and even subnormal children, and it

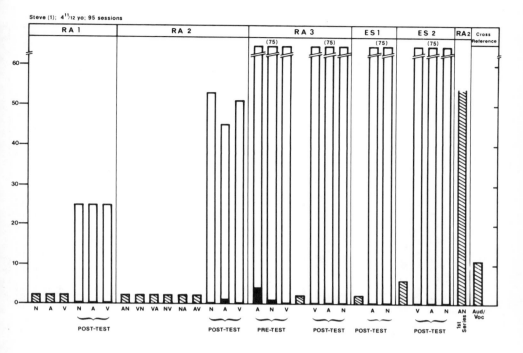

Steve (1); 4^{11}/12 yo; 95 sessions

FIG. 30. Steve's histogram (1). (For legend, see Figs. 2 and 5.)

is the departure from this kind of performance which is of special interest
with autistic children.

There are a few observations in Steve's training and testing which have
some interest in and of themselves. First, due to an undetected planning error,
Steve's sequence of training proceeded directly from RA1-nouns to RA2
without his first having been exposed to either the adjective or verb portions
of the RA1 task. Thus, over a series of 18 sessions (54 blocks of 25 trials) he
was presented with adjective-noun combinations without ever reaching
criterion (Fig. 30: RA2, 1st series). When the program error was discovered,
we were not even sure if Steve knew his colors to begin with! On
backtracking, Steve learned the RA1-adjective and RA1-verb tasks immediately,
and he subsequently met criterion on all RA2 tasks in minimum time.

Whether Steve indeed did not know his colors previously, or whether he
was simply locked into a rigid "set" on the first RA2 training sequence, is
unclear. However, an examination of his error pattern over these relatively
unproductive 54 blocks of 25 trials is interesting, because his errors occurred

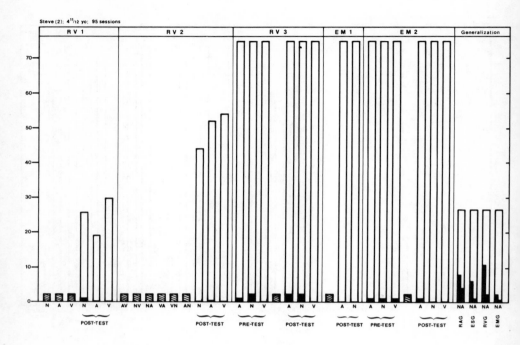

FIG. 31. Steve's histogram (2). (For legend, see Figs. 2 and 5.)

almost exclusively on adjectives. Toward the end of this training sequence, he did show improvement—in fact, approached criterion—but only after he first broke up his rigid error pattern (missing adjectives only) and began for the first time to make noun-only errors. Just as with many of the autistic children, it appears that beginning to make new kinds of mistakes may presage task mastery. This is displayed graphically in the following chart (Fig. 32).

On the four generalization tests, Steve made between 76% and 96% correct responses, thus displaying rather good ability to generalize from the specific objects with which he had been trained (see Fig. 31). And again as observed with highly verbal autistic children, some errors were scored because of too-specific, albeit accurate, responses to the test object. Also, on all four tests, he displayed the familiar pattern of making more errors in response to noun stimuli than in response to adjective stimuli. Once again, it is presumed that this can be most easily explained in terms of the greater similarity of stimulus properties to the original test objects for those items requiring an adjective response as compared to those objects requiring a noun response.

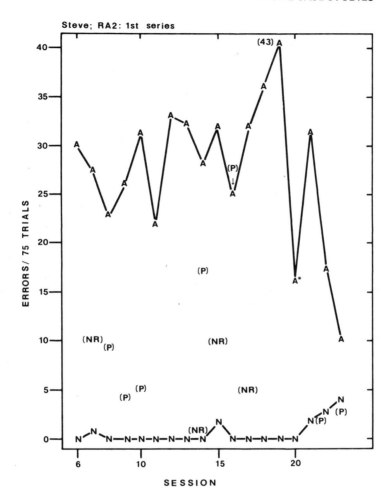

FIG. 32. Steve: Receptive Auditory 2-word task (RA2), first series. A = adjective; A* = sticks only, three colors; (NR) = no response; (P) = prompted correct response.

Lastly, Steve was trained on only one cross-referencing task, i.e., that using an auditory discriminative stimulus and requiring a vocal response (see Fig. 30). The data show steady progress across four sessions until he reached criterion, followed by a post-test of 75 trials in which he made no errors at all.

Shortly thereafter, due to clinical improvement, Steve left our program for another more suited to his needs.

MANUEL

Manuel was 6 years and 3 months of age at the midpoint of testing with the 9WL. He had been diagnozed as subnormal (mentally retarded) rather than autistic, and he had been hospitalized principally for behavioral problems—in particular, severe tantrums and banging his head when he did not get his way. He had some low level speech for communication. His Vineland Social Quotient was 40. On the Peabody Picture Vocabulary test, his IQ was 18. On the Cattell-Binet, his IQ was 33. His social rating was 1–2, i.e., he was either overly friendly or clinging, with too little inhibition in relation to strangers, or he would have stormy relationships with those who did not give into his demands. He had considerable capacity for giving and receiving affection.

On follow-up at 11 years of age, he was found to have speech for his immediate needs and would answer "who" questions, but he could not really converse. A behavioral relapse at home had resulted in institutionalization. He was reported to be a bit more affectionate. He could not be contained in a classroom but was receiving some tutoring. He could count to nine by rote, and there was some recognition of printed words without apparent understanding of meaning.

Manuel had 169 training sessions with the 9WL, the third highest of all the children. Yet, there was no particular spot at which he was found to be irretrievably stuck; everything just took a bit longer. Also, in general, except for his displaying especial difficulty in mastering tasks involving colors (adjectives), his errors tended to be diffuse and unfocused. The sequence effect, so pronounced with some autistic children, was barely evident (on RV3), and there were no particular modality problems. The sessions were often stormy, and there would be periods with rather high rates of nonresponding, which appeared to us clinically to be part of Manuel's general struggle to control situations.

As seen in Figure 33, Manuel required an extraordinary amount of training only on the adjective portion of the RA1 task, but once criterion was met he completed the post-test without error. On the RA2 test, he required up to 30 blocks of 25 trials before reaching criterion, and it is seen that he had especial difficulty with those 2-word combinations which included an adjective. However, by the sixth 2-word sequence (adjective-verb), he mastered the task in scarcely more time than he required for verb-noun and noun-verb combinations. As noted before, the extra training required pertained principally to mastery of adjectives, and there was no strong sequence effect in any of the 2-word combinations. On RA2 post-test, Manuel responded correctly 85% of the time, and there was no discernible pattern to his errors.

Manuel (1); 6 3/12 yo; 169 sessions

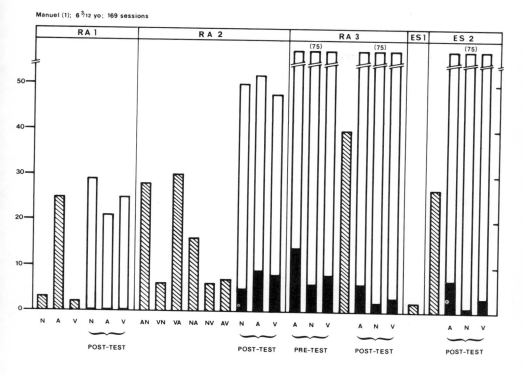

FIG. 33. Manuel's histogram (1). (For legend, see Figs. 2 and 5.)

On the RA3 task, Manuel did not reach criterion until after 40 blocks of 25 trials. This was accomplished only with fixing first the verb and finally the noun in the adjective-noun-verb stimulus sequence. As before, Manuel's error patterns seemed rather diffuse, although he consistently made more errors on adjectives than on other parts of speech. This is reflected not only in his training but in the predominant errors on both pre-test and post-test of the RA3 task. It is also noted that though his performance varied considerably, depending on which adult was working with him (particularly with respect to the number of "no responses"), the preponderance of adjective errors was seen throughout. While in general his error patterns and strategies seemed less consistent than in autistic children, an error pattern did appear in session 86 where, for awhile, he missed only verbs, then only nouns, rather than adjectives.

Manuel met the criterion for the ES1 task in minimum time, giving both noun and adjective responses. The ES2 task tool considerably more training to criterion, principally because of difficulty in establishing a verb response set. Once this was done, Manuel would regularly say the appropriate verb and, interestingly, the adjective rather than the noun. On post-test he made only 10 errors (87% correct responding), but 7 of these errors were on adjectives.

On turning to the RV1 task, Manuel mastered nouns and verbs in scarcely more than minimum time. In contrast, he progressed very slowly on adjectives even after the stimulus array was limited to objects of only one shape at a time. Although trained beyond the usual cut-off point of 42 blocks of 25 trials, Manuel had still not reached criterion on adjectives when the RV1 post-test was given. There, although doing well overall, his special difficulty with adjectives is again reflected (Fig. 34).

On the RV2 task, Manuel was trained for 35 blocks of 25 trials before reaching criterion on the adjective-noun combination. Thereafter, he seemed to "catch on" and reached criterion on the remaining five 2-word combinations in 2 to 4 blocks of 25 trials. The RV2 post-test reflects good overall mastery of the RV2 task. Adding an additional word on the RV3 task required only a little extra training to criterion; and again the post-test shows good mastery of the task except for the familiar preponderance of adjective errors. By this time, however, the peak of errors on adjectives probably represents a sequence effect rather than particular difficulty with adjectives per se, since through a procedural error all RV3 training sessions employed the verb-adjective-noun sequence (wherein Manuel's errors occurred primarily on verbs) and on the post-test the sequence was inadvertently changed to the adjective-noun-verb sequence. In other words, Manuel appears finally to have thoroughly mastered the three adjectives. In fact, he had done it all at once, so to speak, while working on the RV2-AN task. However, under the input load of three words in succession, he began to show for the first time a slight sequence effect which had not been apparent with 2-word combinations.

On the EM1 task, Manuel got off to a slow start. Presented with a new task, he resisted motor prompts and tantrummed in the first session until it was stopped. In the following sessions, his correct responses in successive blocks of 25 trials were 0, 1, 5, 5, 18, 24, 19, 21, 25. Thus, once behavioral control was gained, his correct responses climbed precipitously, and the task was ended with a high level of stable, correct responding. An interesting detail is that although prompted in learning this response to give both noun and adjective responses, in the last two sessions he completely dropped adjective responses and made exclusively noun responses, always correctly. Later, when presented with the EM2 task, in which he was required to make a correct verb plus a noun *or* adjective response, he learned quickly but never made an

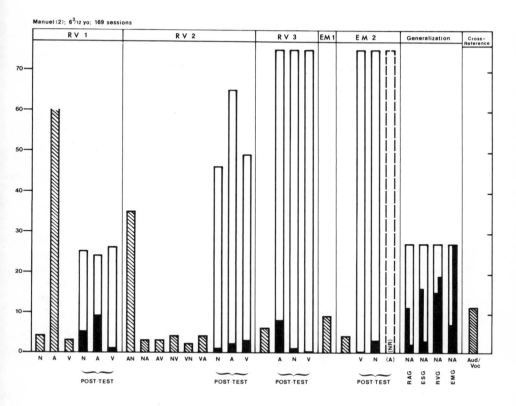

FIG. 34. Manuel's histogram (2). (For legend, see Figs. 2 and 5.)

adjective response. This is again reflected on the post-test: All of his responses were verb + noun.

On the first two generalization tests, Manuel showed a preponderance of noun errors over adjective errors on the RAG and ESG. He seemed to work diligently, as evidenced by his often selecting the wrong object on the RAG, seeming to recognize this before placing it in the box, and successfully correcting himself. Several of his errors on the ESG were similar to those of high-functioning autistic children: He would correctly name an object, e.g., "wheel, wheel, wheel," which indeed it was but which would be scored as an error. In contrast, on the last two generalization tests, RVG and EMG, Manuel made preponderantly adjective errors. During the RVG, some behavior appeared to interfere with successful performance in particular ways. For instance, responding to the sign for *red*, he would imitate the sign, vocalize "ree" (Manuel's pronounciation of *ring*), and place a ring in the box; or else he might imitate the *red* sign plus the *block* sign and word, and then put a block in the box. In other words, his penchant was for responding to the shapes rather than to the colors of objects. On the final generalization test, EMG, he made fewer noun errors than he had previously on the ESG, but now he made very few adjective responses and none of them were correct. This might well reflect the same set he had displayed on the EM2 post-test administered 9 days previously. At any rate, the rather strong selective inattention to colors, in spite of the fact that Manuel had in fact mastered the colors in question, remains as an interesting but puzzling observation.

Manuel's last work with the 9WL consisted of 11 cross-referencing sessions using an auditory discriminative stimulus and a vocal response. Within 11 blocks of 25 trials, he was making 0 to 2 errors per block. His performance remained almost as good when novel objects were used in the same task.

Comparing Manuel's performance on the 9WL with that of autistic children, it appears that aside from his taking longer to master most tasks involving adjectives, he displayed no special modality problems. Yet, he was a bit slower at almost everything than most autistic children, who appear in at least one or two areas to master these tasks in minimum time. Not reflected in the histogram, but evident from behavioral notes, Manuel also displayed more disturbed behavior (tantrumming, teasing, blatant noncooperation) and nonresponding than did any of the autistic children tested. On the other hand, there was less withdrawn and ritualistic behavior. Error patterns, such as the sequence effect, are much less evident, and "strategies" are not as easy to discern.

EARL

Earl was 5 years and 3 months of age at the midpoint of his work with the 9WL. He was transferred from a state hospital and admitted to the research unit because he was homeless, there was a lack of appropriate placement, and the hospital had difficulty managing disturbed behavior which included rather severe tantrums and head-beating. Earl had considerable speech for communication at the time of admission. He was never considered an autistic child, but rather was subnormal (mentally retarded) with associated behavioral and emotional problems. His adaptive quotient was 36, verbal quotient 24. His work with the 9WL covered a period of 4 months and involved 91 sessions. No follow-up information is available.

Earl moved through the receptive auditory and expressive speech portions of the 9WL without hesitation. On all RA1 and RA2 tasks, he reached criterion in minimum time and his post-tests, as depicted in Figure 35, display the fact that he made practically no errors.

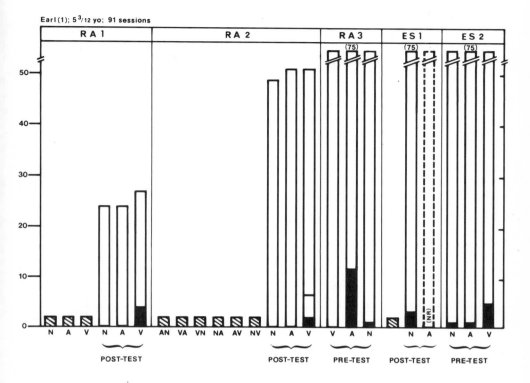

FIG. 35. Earl's histogram (1). (For legend, see Figs. 2 and 5.)

One minor curiosity is that on five trials of the RA2 post-test he responded to either a noun-adjective or adjective-noun stimulus by responding to both parts correctly but then added an "uncalled for" verb response on his own. Because of his immediate mastery of both RA1 and RA2 tasks, preliminary training in the RA3 tasks was omitted. Instead, he simply was pre-tested with 75 randomized trials using a verb-adjective-noun sequence. Here he made no first element (verb) errors, but he did respond incorrectly to the adjective element on 12 of the 75 trials. He made only one noun error. On the ES1 task he again immediately demonstrated competence, reaching criterion in minimum time. On the ES1 post-test, while Earl could have responded to the objects presented with a noun or an adjective or both, all of his responses were nouns. He volunteered no adjective responses. This predilection is interesting in view of his differential errors on the RA3 post-test, where he made only 1 noun error but 12 adjective errors. It is also reminiscent of the

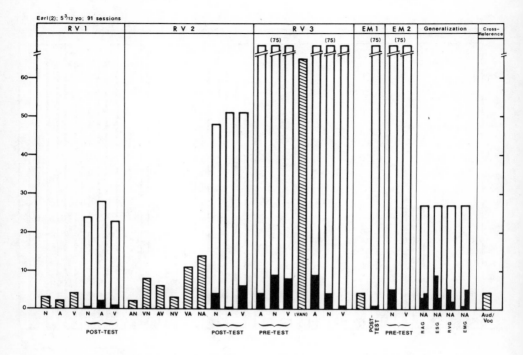

FIG. 36. Earl's histogram (2). (For legend, see Figs. 2 and 5.)

selective responding of another subnormal child, *Manuel*. On the ES2 task, preliminary training was again omitted in favor a pre-test. Once again, Earl's errors are rare (as shown in Figure 35).

When presented with the RV1 task, Earl again reached criterion quickly. It is curious that he did slightly better here on adjectives, the part of speech which had caused him most difficulty in receptive auditory tasks. On a randomized post-test, he then made only 3 errors in 75 trials, 2 adjective errors, and 1 verb error (Fig. 36).

Although not shown in this sequence in Figure 36, Earl was given the RAG before moving next to the EM1 task, where he reached criterion in just 4 blocks of 25 trials. On the post-test, he made a single adjective error. In 75 trials, he responded 43 times with an adjective alone and 32 times with an adjective plus a noun. Never did he respond with a noun alone. This again represents a curious shift from his previous response pattern on the ES1 post-test, where he made only noun responses and no adjective responses. No relationship between stimulus object (color or shape) and his responding either with an adjective or an adjective plus a noun could be discerned. Earl next was given the EMG before moving on to the RV2 task.

It is on the RV2 task that Earl, for the first time, showed some increased difficulty in reaching criterion. To reach criterion on all of the six 2-word combinations required 45 blocks of 25 trials, or 1,125 trials (compared to 12 blocks of 25 trials, or 300 trials, on the RA2 task), and when these 2-word combinations were mixed he had another 52 blocks of training before being given the post-test. Thus, overall he had 97 blocks of 25 trials (2,425 training trials) before being given the RV2 post-test. It would appear, then, that like other subnormal children who were given the 9WL, Earl had special difficulty neither with parts of speech nor with particular channels or modalities, but rather with "input overload" of some sort—possibly a limitation of visual memory. It was as if we were simply giving Earl too many bits of information for him to respond to at once, and the result was protracted training together with the first appearance of emotional outbursts and behavioral disruption during the 9WL. But this very "learning problem" also gave us our first glimpse at Earl's error patterns and learning strategies. For he made almost all of his errors initially on the first element of the stimulus, and, on the correction trial immediately following, he tended to change both the first and second elements, so that although now he was responding correctly to the first element, he also had introduced a new error on the second element. Toward the end of Earl's RV2 training, as his performance began to improve, we once again saw a gradual decline in first element errors and an increase in second element errors until, finally, his errors were distributed rather evenly across both elements. This is depicted in Table 19.

This even distribution of errors across the first and second stimulus elements in the last 300 trials was seen also in the post-test where Earl made errors on 9 of the 75 trials: 4 errors on the first element of the 2-word stimulus, 4 errors on the second element of the 2-word stimulus, and 1 error

Table 19. Earl: Receptive Visual 2-Word Task (RV2) Errors

	First element errors	Second element errors
All RV2 training (2,425 trials)	289	57
First 300 trials	57	2
Last 300 trials	15	13

involving both stimulus elements. Looked at by part of speech (and portrayed in Figure 36), these errors were made in relation to four nouns, no adjectives, and six verbs. These noun and verb errors were made when those parts of speech occupied both the first and second elements of the 2-word stimulus. Thus, at this rather high level of mastery, Earl was making no adjective errors, a few errors on verbs and nouns, and was attending about equally to the first and second elements of the 2-word stimulus. Stated differently, Earl's error pattern—when tasks became difficult enough for it to emerge—was *diffuse* and, in seeming distinction from autistic children, showed no pattern according to part of speech, sensory modality, etc.

Earl was next given an EM2 pre-test. In contrast to the EM1 post-test, where he made adjective rather than noun responses, on this EM2 test he made all verb and noun responses and no adjective responses. Because he made only 5 noun errors (plus 6 verb omissions) in 75 trials, he was given no further work on this task. Instead, the task was shifted to RV3.

On pre-testing, Earl made a total of 19 errors on the RV3 pre-tests 2 adjectives, 7 nouns, 8 verbs, and 2 adjective-noun combinations. Our attention then turned to RV3 training, wherein Earl did not reach criterion until after 65 blocks of 25 trials (1,625 trials), after which a post-test resulted in 14 errors overall—about the same as he had made before the extensive training. The shift in distribution of errors between pre-test and post-test on the RV3 task, while overall errors remain about the same, is displayed in Figure 36 and again might be construed as a sequence effect supporting the notion that his limitation is related to visual memory or "input overload" rather than to modality or part of speech.

This sequence effect while Earl was working on the RV3 task is also shown in Table 20. Following the RV3 pre-test, there was a month hiatus before training continued. When it was resumed, there was an inadvertent shift from

Table 20. Receptive Visual 3-Word Task (RV3) Sequence Effect

Sequence	Sessions	Errors	Stimulus element		
			1st	*2nd*	*3rd*
VAN	82–84	Total	48	27	2
		Mean	16	9	.7
ANV	86–88	Total	32	14	4
		Mean	10.7	4.7	1.3

the adjective-noun-verb sequence presented on the pre-test to a verb-adjective-noun sequence. Toward the end of training, just before the RV3 post-test, the altered sequence was noticed, and the training sequence was restored to adjective-noun-verb. Looking at the errors in relation to the sequence, we see that regardless of the part of speech involved the number of errors is related to the distance between the stimulus and the response (and intervening stimuli) rather than to the part of speech.

Looking through the RV3 training trial-by-trial discloses no particular error patterns other than this sequence effect. In contrast to some autistic children, Earl did not get into long sequences of consecutive errors on his training trials. When confronted with an error, he changed his response to just a single element of the three-part stimulus rather than (as he had earlier) changing his entire response and thereby introducing new errors while correcting the old one.

Earl was given each of the four generalization tests just after he had finished the RA1, ES1, RV1, and EM1 tasks, respectively. He scored a number of errors on each task, often for nonresponding, although his correct responses indicate some definite ability to generalize the 9WL learning on each of the four tasks. The differences in his errors on nouns vs. adjectives are similar to those seen in other children.

Earl's last work with the 9WL involved the cross-referencing task, using an auditory discriminative stimulus and a vocal response. Within 4 blocks of 25 trials he had reached criterion, and he continued another 125 trials without error. This indicates, at least for these modalities, that this subnormal child was able to make a differential vocal response to overlapping properties of a visual stimulus, using an auditory discriminative stimulus. It may be noteworthy that although Earl, a subnormal child, had a great deal more trouble on RV3 than did an autistic child (*Leon*), he mastered the cross-referencing task with ease, whereas *Leon* found that task impossible. While both had good speech, Earl used if for communication; *Leon* did not.

CHAPTER 5

FINAL CONSIDERATIONS

By this time, there can be little room for doubt that all of the autistic children investigated with the experimental 9-word language and other procedures described in this book were suffering from a severe language defect. In retrospect, it is unfortunate that more of the highest functioning autistic children were not investigated more extensively beyond the conditioning and simple association (9WL) level of language function. The early development and use of the 9WL so absorbed our interest and resources that the significance of equally detailed investigation of more complex language function was not appreciated until shortly before the Research Unit was closed. The fact that Orson, Curtis, and Edgar all demonstrated marked discrepancies on the performance vs. verbal portions of the WISC when later tested (31, 57, and 42 IQ points, respectively) suggests that these children, too, would have been found to display difficulties as had Jonathan and Leon.

The lower functioning autistic children are marked, in one way or another, by some defect in their basic conditionability which, in turn, precludes the establishment of a full range of reliable precision skills that must serve as a foundation for full language development. This is made clear by their various difficulties in mastering the 9WL grid. But even those middle- and high-functioning autistic children who easily mastered the 9WL are also found, on detailed examination, with progressively higher language functions to reveal their own special language deficits which can scarcely be less deleterious with respect to the development of useful language. The point is that none are spared, neither the mute nor the highly verbal. Bartak and Rutter (1976), comparing autistic children with nonverbal IQs greater than and less than 70, reported that the basic features of autism appeared in both, and that the similarities between the groups outweighed the dissimilarities but that nonverbal IQ was an important indicator of educational and work prognosis. Such might be some of the long-range effect of the differences found in the lower and higher functioning children studied here. Prior, Perry, and Gajzago (1975) used a multivariant analysis of slightly modified Rimland E-2 forms on 142 psychotic children in Australia, two-thirds of whom had no communicative speech. The resultant "best" classification divided the group into early and later onset types, with slightly less than half of the former groups scoring above 17 on the E-2 form. The other portion of this first group was also nonrelating and had fewer fine motor skills and other "islets of ability." Thus, it seems likely that we are again looking at autistic children who can be distinguished on the basis of greater and lesser nonverbal skills. While the children described in Prior et al.'s study were not characterized with respect to communication skills, it is possible that the lower and higher functioning autistic children would also be characterized by the absence or presence, respectively, of basic conditionability.

But even if autistic children can be broadly classified into two groups according to the level at which language deficits can be detected, and which are in broad accord with lower and higher overall functioning, the uniqueness of each autistic child's language problem must be kept in mind. The lack of communicative speech or gesture is conspicuous in all, but each seems to be blocked in a special way. This is very clear in chapter 4, where children's work is individually scrutinized. And what is perhaps most important from the clinical standpoint at present is that wherever an autistic child reaches an impasse, be he low functioning or high, it seems virtually impossible to find a way past this impasse. From the child's side, we can find no evidence of avoiding or of not trying. Indeed, the opposite is true: We see intelligence, strategies, and simple experimentation. Still, with the best efforts of child and adult alike, they both stay stuck. This raises some issues concerning treatment strategy and prognosis.

First, as in any intractible illness or developmental disability, there are recurrent reports of new breakthroughs. A current one is the use of American Sign Language or other forms of manual communication to communicate with autistic children. Since the handicaps of individual autistic children are so varied, it is quite likely that certain ones can benefit more from visual-motor modes of communication than from auditory-vocal. For such children, a better resource will have been tapped, and it may be expected that they can then be helped to hitherto unrecognized limits. But this is not to say that the underlying language problem is circumvented. The data presented here would strongly suggest that the impasse will simply be found in another place, most likely in higher levels of language function. The same can be said for the, by now, very extensive efforts to teach speech for communication through operant conditioning. That much can be done is not in doubt. The critical question is whether, once having established basic precision skills through conditioning, an autistic child can be led into generative speech (or hand signs), i.e., the ability to both understand and to generate novel sentences beyond those to which he has been trained. All clinicians strain to see this as the result of their work, and yet the reports are not convincing. Thus, in the Stevens-Long and Rasmussen (1974) training of the child to speak compound as well as simple sentences there is no evidence that their subject is doing more in his "generative" sentences than simply chaining previously trained responses via a conjunctive "and" response, also trained. Similarly, in a report by Freeman, Ritvo, and Miller (1975) in which an autistic child was trained to "answer questions appropriately," it cannot be concluded that the child is "answering" questions at all. No more can be said than that he has been conditioned to make an auditory-vocal or—more likely—visual-vocal response to 40 stimulus pictures. The work presented here, with Jonathan and Leon in particular, indicates how difficult it is to move from trained responses to language even in fully conditionable autistic children, given the types of defects described. Competence with syntax and grammatical transformations are the limiting factors eventually, and at this time the key must be said to lie within the child, not his helper: Those few autistic children who appear to progress furthest in language development do so by virtue of inherent developmental factors rather than training wizardry.

Pierce and Bartolucci (1977), recently investigating syntax in matched groups of verbal autistic, mentally retarded, and normal children, found the autistic children to have extreme developmental language delay plus impaired ability, even beyond that of mentally retarded children, with respect to "linguistic rules." Despite this, the syntax of autistic children was rule governed, which would again accord with our observations: The speech of autistic children, even when noncommunicative or "incorrect," is not simply random or chaotic; we see strategies and patterned errors. Prior (1977), in a roughly confirmatory replication of work by Tubbs (1966), again found both high and low autistic children to be superior to mentally retarded control groups in auditory sequential memory on the Illinois Test of Psycho-linguistic Ability, while both verbal and motor expression was extremely low. Tubbs had noted that tasks requiring spontaneous output and cross-modal coding were especially difficult for autistic children. Comparing the performance of just 3 non-autistic children on the 9WL with 13 autistic children does not provide ground for confident generalizations. However, of the children studied, the non-autistic ones (Steve, Manuel, and Earl) displayed none of the impasses, none of the problems with basic conditionability, that were seen in low-functioning autistic children. This is not to say they were much easier to train; in general, they were slower to learn new tasks, but they did not become so absolutely stuck, and they seemed to reach the limits of their abilities in terms of "capacity" to handle only so much information at once, rather than through specific modality deficits. In contrast, it was more likely to be "easy or impossible" to teach new tasks to the autistic child—depending on the task.

All autistic children can learn *something*, given the proper training conditions. That is not in question. The question rather is, "What are the deficits revealed by systematic training/testing to the limits of an autistic child's ability?" And once the deficits are identified, can they be overcome or circumvented?

I have argued that language deficits of the sort described in this book are the necessary and sufficient cause of those phenomena common to all autistic children, while other types of disabilities (perceptual, visual memory, etc.) might account for some of the differences among autistic children (Churchill, 1972, 1978). Others, both before and since, have also emphasized the importance of language disability in autistic children but have been unwilling to grant it the same central importance (Hermelin, 1968; Pronovost, 1961; Rutter, 1965, 1978b; Wing, 1969). I have done so in an effort to force clarity. The literature now increasingly appends other cognitive factors to those of language in discussions of the essential problem in autism. For example, Boucher (1976) has recently maintained that autism is not primarily a language disorder at all, but argues rather for an underlying "cognitive deficit" of which language impairment is one manifestation. Boucher argues that if autism were primarily a language disorder all children with a verbal IQ below a certain point would be expected to be autistic—which is not the case. Further, some autistic children have relatively high verbal IQ scores, e.g., in the range of educable retarded children. However, the verbal IQ is a global measure poorly suited to detect the language deficits in verbal autistic children. Indeed, that is the whole point of undertaking the studies reported here. The deficits are there to be seen when autistic children are investigated in this way. For me, they look like disorders of language. To argue for or against an underlying cognitive deficit seems rather fruitless until we have better operationalized our definitions of "language" and "cognition."

Table 21. Diagnostic Category and Level of Functioning

CHILDREN			MEASURING INSTRUMENTS							
Rank ordering and diagnosis		Rank	Vineland Social Quotient	Adaptive Quotient*	Peabody Picture Vocabulary	Verbal Quotient*	Draw-A-Person	Cattell-Binet	Stanford-Binet	WISC (P) (V) (FS)
Autistic	*Nonautistic*									
		120								
Orson		110								Orson (P)
Curtis										Curtis (P)
Edgar	Steve (aphasic, mild MR)	100								Edgar (P)
Edward		90								Orson (FS)
Leon										Steve (P)
Betsy		80	Edgar		Edgar		Betsy		Edgar	Edgar (FS)
			Leon							Curtis (FS)
			Curtis, Edward							Edward (P)
			Steve							Orson (V)
		70							Edward	Steve (FS)
										Steve (V)
										Edward (V)
Stan		60		Earl	Leon		Jonathan	Curtis, Leon		Edward (V*)
Jonathan					Edward					Curtis (V)
Louis†										
Earl and Manuel (subnormal, MR)		50			Stan, Betsy, Curtis, Jonathan			Carl, Steve, Andrew	Stan	
		40	Stan	Earl		Steve		Manuel	Jonathan	
Andrew			Manuel			Earl				
Jane†		30	Andrew					Charles		
Carl		20	Charles		Manuel					
Charles		10								

†Individual case data not reported herein.

*DeMyer, Barton, and Norton (1972).

131

REFERENCES

Bartak, L., & Rutter, M. The use of personal pronouns by autistic children. *Journal of Autism and Childhood Schizophrenia*, 1974, **4**, 217–222.

Bartak, L., & Rutter, M. Differences between mentally retarded and normally intelligent autistic children. *Journal of Autism and Childhood Schizophrenia*, 1976, **6**, 109–120.

Benoroya, S., Wesley, S., Ogilvie, H., Klein, L. S., & Meaney, M. Sign language and multisensory input training of children with communication and related developmental disorders. *Journal of Autism and Childhood Schizophrenia*, 1977, **7**, 23–31.

Bonvillian, J. D., & Nelson, K. E. Sign language acquisition in a mute autistic boy. *Journal of Speech and Hearing Disorders*, 1976, **41**, 339–347.

Boucher, J. Is autism primarily a language disorder? *British Journal of Disorders of Communication*, 1976, **11**, 135–143.

Churchill, D. W. Psychotic children and behavior modification. *American Journal of Psychiatry*, 1969, **125**, 1585–1590.

Churchill, D. W. Effects of success and failure in psychotic children. *Archives of General Psychiatry*, 1971, **25**, 208–214.

Churchill, D. W. The relation of infantile autism and early childhood schizophrenia to developmental language disorders of childhood. *Journal of Autism and Childhood Schizophrenia*, 1972, **2**, 182-197.

Churchill, D. W. Language of autistic children: the problem beyond conditioning. In M. Rutter & E. Schopler (Eds.), *Autism: A reappraisal of concepts and treatment*, New York: Plenum, 1978.

DeMyer, M. K., Barton, S., & Norton, J. A. A comparison of adaptive, verbal and motor profiles of psychotic and non-psychotic subnormal children. *Journal of Autism and Childhood Schizophrenia*, 1972, **2**, 359-377.

DeMyer, M. K., Churchill, D. W., Pontius, W., & Gilkey, K. M. A comparison of five diagnostic systems for childhood schizophrenia and infantile autism. *Journal of Autism and Childhood Schizophrenia*, 1971, **1**, 175-189.

Freeman, B. J., Ritvo, E., & Miller, R. An operant procedure to teach an echolalic autistic child to answer questions appropriately. *Journal of Autism and Childhood Schizophrenia*, 1975, **5**, 169-176.

Hermelin, B. Recent experimental research. In P. J. Mittler (Ed.), *Aspects of autism*. London: British Psychological Society, 1968.

Hingtgen, J. N., & Churchill, D. W. Identification of perceptual limitations in mute autistic children. *Archives of General Psychiatry*, 1969, **21**, 68-71.

Hingtgen, J. N., Coulter, S. K., & Churchill, D. W. Intensive reinforcement of imitative behavior in mute autistic children. *Archives of General Psychiatry*, 1967, **17**, 36-43.

Kanner, L. Autistic disturbances of affective contact. *The Nervous Child*, 1943, **2**, 217-250.

Kolvin, I. Studies in the childhood psychoses. *British Journal of Psychiatry*, 1971, **118**, 381-385.

Mark, H. J. Psychodiagnostics in patients with suspected minimal brain dysfunction(s). In *Minimal brain dysfunction in children* (Public Health Service Publication No. 2015). Washington, D.C.: U.S. Government Printing Office, 1969.

Miller, A., & Miller, E. E. Cognitive developmental training with elevated boards and sign language. *Journal of Autism and Childhood Schizophrenia*, 1973, **3**, 65-85.

Pierce, S., & Bartolucci, G. A syntactic investigation of verbal autistic, mentally retarded, and normal children. *Journal of Autism and Childhood Schizophrenia*, 1977, **7**, 121-134.

Prior, M. R. Psycholinguistic disabilities of autistic and retarded children. *Journal of Mental Deficiency Research*, 1977, **21**, 37-45.

Prior, M., Perry, D., & Gajzago, C. Kanner's syndrome or early onset psychosis: A taxonomic analysis of 142 cases. *Journal of Autism and Childhood Schizophrenia*, 1975, **5**, 71-80.

Pronovost, W. The speech and language comprehension of autistic children. *Journal of Chronic Diseases*, 1961, **13**, 228-233.

Risley, T., & Wolf, M. Establishing functional speech in echolalic children. *Behavior Research and Therapy*, 1967, **5**, 73-88.

Rutter, M. Speech disorders in a series of autistic children. In A. W. Franklin (Ed.), *Children with communication problems*. London: Pitman, 1965.

Rutter, M. Concepts of autism: A review of research. *Journal of Child Psychology and Psychiatry*, 1968, **9**, 1–25.

Rutter, M. The description and classification of infantile autism. In D. Churchill, G. Alpern, & M. DeMyer (Eds.), *Infantile autism: Proceedings of the Indiana University Colloquium*. Springfield, Illinois: Charles C Thomas, 1971.

Rutter, M. Clinical characteristics of autism. In M. Rutter & E. Schopler (Eds.), *Autism: A reappraisal of concepts and treatment*. New York: Plenum, 1978. (a)

Rutter, M. Language disorder and infantile autism. In M. Rutter & E. Schopler (Eds.), *Autism: A reappraisal of concepts and treatment*. New York: Plenum, 1978. (b)

Stevens-Long, J., & Rasmussen, M. The acquisition of simple and compound sentences in an autistic child. *Journal of Applied Behavior Analysis*, 1974, **7**, 473–479.

Tubbs, V. K. Types of linguistic disability in psychotic children. *Journal of Mental Deficiency Research*, 1966, **10**, 230–240.

Webster, C. D., McPherson, H., Sloman, L., Evans, M. A., & Kuchar, E. Communicating with an autistic boy by gestures. *Journal of Autism and Childhood Schizophrenia*, 1973, **3**, 337–346.

Wing, L. The handicaps of autistic children—a comparative study. *Journal of Child Psychology and Psychiatry*, 1969, **10**, 1–40.

SUBJECT/CONCEPT INDEX